LIVE THEATRE

D1301243

Four Plays for Young People
by

C. P. TAYLOR

A Methuen New Theatrescript
Methuen London/ IRON Press

A METHUEN PAPERBACK

This collection first published in 1983 as a Methuen Paperback original by Methuen London Ltd, 11 New Fetter Lane, London EC4P 4EE, in association with IRON Press, 5 Marden Terrace, Cullercoats, North Shields, Tyne & Wear NE30 4PD

The Magic Island, Operation Elvis and *The Rainbow Coloured Disco Dancer* originally published in one volume by IRON Press in 1981.

The Magic Island, Operation Elvis, The Rainbow Coloured Disco Dancer
copyright © C.P. Taylor 1981
Happy Lies copyright © 1983 by the Estate of the late C.P. Taylor

Typeset by Tyneside Free Press Workshop, 5 Charlotte Square, Newcastle upon Tyne.
Printed in Great Britain by Richard Clay (The Chaucer Press) Ltd, Bungay, Suffolk

ISBN 0 413 51790 X

Contents

Author's Note

The plays in this volume are the latest in a series of plays coming out of a long-term children's theatre project on Tyneside, which began in 1972 and which has recently moved into work with the mentally handicapped.

Since the stumbling beginnings, I have refined the techniques that I describe as *'tuning into an audience'*. I use several approaches to give me an understanding of the children, their culture and subculture all basically leading to a good two-way, mutually respectful relationship with them.

(1) Written work. Both day-to-day classwork and specially set work, e.g. a diary of their week, Two Wishes, etc.

(2) Two-to-One and one-to-one interviews. I try to make these as searching and challenging as possible. The interview begins with relatively reassuring questions, sisters, friends, mothers and father, moving on to more dangerous ground—fears, anxieties, self-images, resentments . . .

(3) I take some of the children on walkabouts round where they live, where they play, favourite shops, etc.

(4) I visit a few parents and find out what kind of home the children live in, what kind of people their parents are.

(5) I bring in an actor, actors, directors, to do some drama work with the class, partly designed to reveal attitudes that have not come out of direct interviews. I might ask them to act out family situations, their day. Or simply exercise their imagination on an old known story.

Through all these processes, hopefully, I have some authority to claim an understanding of the children, their preoccupations, the emotional currents running in the group, conflicts, and their general level of understanding and development. Usually some theme in particular will have emerged and the experience has triggered off my creative unconscious.

By the end of my period of work with the children, wherever the school might have been, my main response is always the basic human response, of course. I end up liking the kids, enjoying the time spent with them and aware of their potential much of which, alas, is unlikely to ever be realised.

I try to make my plays for children as rewarding for adults so that they can be the shared experience all good theatre is. I have been accused of over-estimating the intelligence and understanding of the children. Perhaps at times I do. I don't worry about this too much. There are enough people *under*-estimating them at the present time, and it does seem to me that children, or rather most people, are as clever or as stupid as you expect them to be.

C.P. Taylor,
Northumberland 1981

Operation Elvis

CAST LIST

*First performed on tour in Newcastle, January 1978
with the following cast.*

Malcolm: Tim Healy
Dad:
Headmaster: Max Roberts
Jackie:
Mother:
Sister: Denise Bryson
Lynn:
Michael: Brian Hogg

Directed by Teddy Kiendl
Designed by Phil Bailey

MALCOLM:	*(IN ELVIS GEAR)* WELL it's one for the money, two for the show, Three to get ready, now go Cat go, But don't you Step on my blue suede shoes. You can do anything But lay off my blue suede shoes . . .
	(TO AUDIENCE): What do you think? Good as Elvis, isn't it? That's because that's who I am, Elvis, Elvis Presley . . . I mean, I know I'm Malc Robson, but I'm Elvis Presley, too. You'll see what I mean when I start telling you my story. Well you can burn my house, steal my car, drink my liquor, from my old fruit jar . . .
MAM:	Malc . . . Malc.
MALC:	Do anything that you want to do . . .
MAM:	Have you put me egg on? See, first thing in the morning people can't stand that noise, man . . . Malc
MALC:	But huh honey, lay off my shoes, Don't you step on my blue suede shoes. *(MAM PULLS OUT HIS PLUG, GUITAR AND MIKE GOES DEAD)*
MALC:	I've put your egg on,
MAM:	*(FONDLING HIM)* Listen, pet, you're a good lad, Ye are, aren't you?
MALC:	Yeah, I'm good.
MAM:	Listen, You like Alex, don't you?
MALC:	*(TO AUDIENCE):* Did I? me Dad, see, had an accident in the Naval Yard, when I was two or three . . . He was welding on this ship, I don't know, anyway . . . He died in the hospital . . . I can't remember him.
MALC:	Alex, he's alright.
MAM:	I was thinking I might marry him. What do you think? *(OPENING HER EGG)*
MALC:	Alex?
MAM:	Make another slice of toast, pet. You could do with a father, couldn't you, Malc?

MALC:	*(TO AUD:)* That's me Mam, you see, she's always getting married. Last time it was this Ticket collector on the railway. Took us a free trip to Manchester. I got me dinner on the train. She went off him. Always goes off people.
MAM:	I've made ye an egg, Alex.
ALEX:	Ye not going to school, today?
MALC:	*(TO AUD.)* Alex had an old lorry, went around collecting scrap and junk and that, cannie! Always gave you ten or twenty P. whenever he saw you.
MAM:	He's going in a minute, love.
ALEX:	Like that?
MAM:	That's what I was saying to him, before. It's time he had a proper Dad again, isn't it?
ALEX:	Malc, come here son.
MALC:	I'm getting me things ready. *(ALEX GETS UP AND GOES TO MALC)*
MAM:	Listen to me son. Ye're a good lad, de ye hear me. You are a cannie little lad for yer age. Always helping yer Mam and everything.
MALC:	*(TO AUD.)* That's what started it, I could see his point of view. He couldn't understand how I was Elvis and Malc at the same time.
ALEX:	Listen, Malc, you're *not* Elvis Presley. You can't go about all yer life disguised as Elvis the Pelvis, as they say, can you?
MALC:	*(TO AUD.)* I mean, I'd been through this with dozens of people before, hundreds of times. *(TO ALEX)* . . . I'm Elvis, Alex. I'm Elvis Presley.
ALEX:	Let us look at this sensibly, lad . . . Right? Ye're ten now, in another year ye'll have to go to Hamer Park School, and wear a school uniform and everything. It's time now you stopped being a kid, lad and woke up. You show up at Hamer Park School in them clothes, they'll hoy ye out, won't they?
MALC:	Yeah, I'm Elvis.
ALEX:	How are ye Elvis? Ye're ten years of age, Elvis is dead.
MALC:	That's how. He died. Somebody told us when you die your spirits go into a new baby.
MAM:	Ee, I think there might be something in that. Will you get the marmalade, pet?

7

ALEX:	Malc you're *ten* man. Elvis died *after* you were born. So that's out isn't it?
MAM:	Wait on, Alex, that night, it was on the news. On John Craven's News, that Elvis had died. I cried a bit too. It was like the queen dying or something.
MALC:	His spirit went into us.
ALEX:	Oh, for God's sake, man!
MAM:	Something funny happened, definitely.
ALEX:	Where you going?
MALC:	Gotta to go to school.
ALEX:	Listen, your Mam's told you I'm going to be yer new Dad has she?
MALC:	If you want to?
ALEX:	What do *you* think about it?
MALC:	It's good.
ALEX:	We're good pals, aren't we?
MALC:	Yeah.
ALEX:	Who's the Greatest?
MALC:	Newcastle United.
ALEX:	There you are.
MAM:	Ee, it'll be nice, the two of you going to St. James Park on a Saturday afternoon.
ALEX:	So, I don't want people to think my kid's off his nut or anything do I?
MALC:	No.
ALEX:	Right, do us a favour. go and put some proper clothes on and do your hair like all the other kids.
MALC:	*(TO AUD.)* Difficult, that isn't it? When they're nice to you about it. Like if he'd said "Do that or else". I'll be late.
MAM:	I'll give ye a note. Go on ye'll please both of us, Malc.
MALC:	I'll do it tomorrow.
ALEX:	Today.
MALC:	I'm Elvis.
ALEX:	Ye're not rotten Elvis.
MALC:	I *am*, I *am*, I *am (TO AUD.)* And I grabbed me guitar and just ran out the house before either of them could get a chance to grab us.

MAM:	Malc . . . Malc.
ALEX:	Malc. Come back here, ye rotten little waster.
MALC:	It was dead sunny, I could see the big bridge across the Tyne and all the Gateshead flats and everything. I was standing there like Elvis, you know, all shook up. I hated upsetting me Mam like that but I didn't know what to do. A well bless my soul, what's wrong with me? I'm itching like a man on a fuzzy tree, My friends say I'm acting queer as a bug I'm in love, I'm all shook up.
MALC:	I was just going into the school, making for me class when Frank Sinatra caught us.
MR. GREEN:	Malcolm.
MALC:	*(TO AUD.)* I don't know why I call him Frank Sinatra. He's a dead cannie bloke. Like him. Better than some of the heads I've had. I mean, he doesn't even look like Frank Sinatra.
MALC:	Just going up to the class Mr. Green.
HEAD:	Malcolm, come in a minute I want to speak to you.
HEAD:	Did you give your mother my letter?
MALC:	*(TO AUD.)* His letter, his *letter*. Hells rotten bells! His letter. *(TO HEAD)* Yeah.
HEAD:	And she sent you to school today like this Malcolm. Come on, now. You know better than to treat me like an idiot. What did you do with the letter?
MALC:	*(TO AUD.)* They were always sending letters to me Mam, especially Frank Sinatra. Had a thing about letters. I usually read them meself to her, she couldn't be bothered reading letters.
HEAD:	I'm waiting, Malcolm. What did you do with the letter? *(NO ANSWER)* You read it didn't you Malcolm, and because you didn't want your mother to see it you threw it away. That's it isn't it?
MALC:	*(TO HEAD)* No, I didn't, I always give me Mam your letters, you know that. I remember now, I forgot all about it. It's probably still in me pocket. *(LOOKS AND FINDS IT)* See, it's not opened or anything.
HEAD:	Open it Malcolm. Go on. *(MALCOLM OPENS IT)*
HEAD:	Read it. *(MALCOLM READS SILENTLY)*
HEAD:	Out loud.

MALC: *(READING)* Dear Mrs. Robson, I have written to you on several occasions about Malcolm coming to school unsuitably dressed. The last time we discussed this you assured me this would not continue. However, Malcolm still comes to school in clothes more suitable for an evenings disco than a day's work at school.
I think you will agree we have been extremely patient with Malcolm over this. If you wish to discuss this with me, you know I am available at all times. Yours sincerely.

HEAD: I'm really worried you.

MALC: *(TO AUD.)* That really got us. People worrying. Hate people worrying about us. *(TO HEAD)* Yeah, I'm alright.

HEAD: It seems to me you're getting even worse, Malcolm, this obsession you have for Elvis Presley. You're nearly eleven Malcolm. I remember last year, even, you just turned up odd days in that rock and roll gear of yours. Now it's everyday isn't it? The obsession seems to be getting a bigger and bigger hold on you.
Listen Malcolm everybody has their imagination, their fantasies. You know what fantasies mean?

MALC: Yeah. It's what you want to do but you can't.

HEAD: What seems to be happening to you, but, Malcolm, is that your fantasies are taking over your whole personality more and more, so you lost track of *who* Malcolm Robson is. You understand what I mean? You're beginning to believe you are Elvis Presley.

MALC: I am Elvis Presley.

HEAD: You are not Elvis Presley, you are Malcolm Robson.

MALC: Yeah, I'm Malcolm Robson.

HEAD: Right then, Malcolm, go home and dress like Malcolm Robson.

MALC: I am dressed like him.

HEAD: Malcolm don't argue with me. Go home and put on some normal clothes.

MALC: I'm dressed like Malcolm Robson. Malcolm Robson believes he's Elvis Presley.

HEAD: *(SHOUTING AFTER)* Get out of here Malcolm and come back in twenty minutes in normal clothes like all the other boys in the school. *(MALC GOES, HEAD SHOUTS AFTER HIM)*

HEAD:	And give your mother that letter.
MALC:	*(TO AUD.)* I got out of school sharp. The sun was dead bright now. I went through the hall, you could hear all the kids doing their work. The infants were having choir practice, singing Cum bay Yah. Never sang any songs properly in that school, you know with a beat. It's nowt that song without a beat, is it? No songs are.
	I went out through the playground, nearly walked into a dumper with rubbish from the building site. Didn't know what to do. One thing for sure, I wasn't going back to rotten Raby Street School again.
	Now since my baby left me,
	I've found a new place to dwell,
	Down at the end of Lonely Street,
	At Heartbreak Hotel.
	I'm so lonely, I'm so lonely,
	I'm so lonely that I could die.
JACKIE:	Want a drop scone?
MALC:	Nuh.
JACKIE:	Never heard of George Formby?
MALC:	Nuh.
MALC:	*(TO AUD.)* I ended up at Jackies, didn't know where else to go anyway. You can see, right old nut case, Jackie. Got this pigeon loft on the old railway. Gonna pull it down any minute. Lives in it, I mean. He's got a house in the Wall, but he sleeps in the pigeon house to stop vandals and everybody else knocking down his house and pinching his pigeons. *(TO JACKIE)* What you think I should do, Jackie?
JACKIE:	Want a scone? They're lovely.
MALC:	*(TO AUD.)* Always eating these horrible scones, like bits of rock covered in yellow margarine. Make you sick to watch him scoffing them. *(TO JACKIE)* I don't like scones.
JACKIE:	I might make meself a Ukelele, now come to think of it.
MALC:	I'm sick Jackie. Nobody'll let us be meself.
JACKIE:	See I can't be bothered with rotten pigeons, Elvis. You see, that's it.
MALC:	Sell them.
JACKIE:	If I got rid of them who'd I have left?
MALC:	I mean, *you* believe I'm Elvis Presley.
JACKIE:	If that's who you say you are, son. Do you want a scone?

MALC:	I don't want a scone. I keep telling you I don't like scones.
JACKIE:	Don't know what's good for you.
MALC:	What you reckon I should do, Jackie?
JACKIE:	You not happy here?
MALC:	That's what I am, you're right, I'm not happy.
JACKIE:	*I'm* happy, it's probably the sun, and them scones. I'm always happy eating a good scone and Stork.
MALC:	If they'd leave us alone. You get sick, everyday on to us. *(TO AUD.)*
MALC:	Then he came out with one of his nutcase things. That started the whole thing, he was always doing that.
JACKIE:	What it is, is, you being unhappy, is you're homesick, that's what it is. If George Formby had spent all his life in America that would've been the same thing wouldn't it? He'd have been homesick for Lancashire. You're homesick for New York.
MALC:	New York?
JACKIE:	That's where you come from isn't it? Elvis Pelvis comes from America, doesn't he?
MALC:	Memphis, Tennessee.
JACKIE:	That's it Memphis, Tennessee. Never tried crossing the Atlantic with pigeons. Crossed the channel . . . I never did . It's too big . . . the Atlantic . . . Never get a pigeon across . . Unless they landed on ships every now and then.
MALC:	*(TO AUD.)* I didn't wait to hear the end of his going on about pigeons and the Atlantic. I was running up Shipley Wayback to the house . . . to get my gear and some food for going to Memphis Tennessee. They'd let us be Elvis Presley in Memphis alright, wouldn't they?

> The bellhop's tears keep flowing,
> The desk clerk's dressed in black,
> They've been so long on lonely street,
> They never will go back,
> And they're so lonely, etc.,

(MALC GOES TO THE BACK BEHIND THE SCHOOL AND WHEELS OUT MICHAEL. HE PULLS HIM OUT SO THAT DURING HIS FIRST SPEECH THE AUDIENCE CAN ONLY SEE THE BACK OF THE WHEELCHAIR)

MALC:	*(TO AUD.)* The first time I saw Michael he gave us a funny feeling. I've never had a feeling like that before. I mean it wasn't just him frightening us the way he looked, I couldn't look at him. It was the way his body was all kind of stiff. His face wasn't bad . . . That was his muscles, Lynn told us after, and his slavering, that put you off him too at first. *(HE TURNS THE CHAIR NOW SO THAT MICHAEL FACES THE AUDIENCE . . . TO MICHAEL)*
MALC:	Telling them first time I saw you. *(MICHAEL GRINS . . . TO MICHAEL)*
MALC:	That day I was going to Memphis. *(MICHAEL GESTURES WITH HEAD AND EYES TOWARDS MALC'S GUITAR)*
MALC:	*(TO AUD.)* Yeah, I left a note for me Mam in the house, I'm going home to Memphis. But, I mean, even that day *(TO MICH.)* I didn't really believe I was going to Memphis. *(MICHAEL SMILES)*
MALC:	I didn't . . . I kind of did in a way, but I mean I knew you had to go in a plane an' that across the Atlantic, and the fare would be more than the two pounds seventyfour P I'd taken out of my box, didn't I? *(MICHAEL MAKES A SOUND)*
MALC:	*(TO MICHAEL)* yeah, I know, man they don't know how I found you. I am going to tell them amn't I? See, that was something else. First time I saw him I couldn't understand *him* then. *(TO MICHAEL)* Sounded like a right nut case didn't you? Yah . . . aah . . . ahh . . . gah . . . *(MICHAEL LAUGHS AT MALC'S ATTEMPTS TO IMITATE HIM)*
MALC:	Ended up at Haymarket Bus station, I mean, I just couldn't not go anywhere after leaving that note and saying goodbye to Jackie. So I just jumped on to the first bus I saw. It was going to Morpeth. Be a bit nearer to Memphis wouldn't it? That's how I ended up beside this lake and I met Michael. Everything started there. There was nowt in Morpeth, so I just started walking till I came to green fields and weeds. I'd never been walking in the country before, it was a funny feeling like going into some magic place. The way I found the lake was real magic wasn't it? *(MICHAEL SMILES)*
MALC:	I was crossing this big field till I came to this hedge, dead thick. I kind of forced my way through it . . . and it was going into a magic place. It was fantastic. *(TO MICHAEL)*
MALC:	That day was fantastic, wasn't it? *(MICHAEL LAUGHS)*

MALC: *(TO AUD.)* Birds all singing, flowers everywhere, and trees and through the woods this lake. I couldn't wait to get to it. I ran right through the weeds. It was fantastic, I ran right down a kind of path and tripped. *(HE LOOKS UP AT MICHAEL, TERRIFIED NOW... MICHAEL IS BABBLING. MALC TRIES TO GET UP, BACKING AWAY. MICHAEL CONTINUES TO BABBLE. MICHAEL'S FOOT IN A SPASM TOUCHES HIM AND MALC BACKS AWAY AGAIN)*

MALC: *(TO AUD.)* I got on my feet and started to pick up my guitar and the stuff that had fallen out of my bag. I was just going to run off when I looked at Michael again and he'd kind of slipped to one side of his wheelchair. He was trying to push himself back again but he couldn't. I couldn't leave him like that so I went up to him and helped him to sit straight again. *(TO MICHAEL)*

MALC: There you are, man that's better. *(TO AUD.)* When I looked at his face it was like . . . I've never seen any kid as sad looking as him. His eyes gave us a funny feeling . . . looking at him. *(TO MICHAEL)* What's the matter man, I wasn't going to run away. Just, falling like that, I thought I'd broken my guitar. Do you want a penguin? *(TO AUD.)* All I could think to cheer him up. *(OFFERING HIM A BISCUIT... IT FALLS FROM HIS SPASTIC FINGERS.)*

MALC: Can't hold it . . . Come on, I'll give you it. *(TAKES A BIT OFF AND HOLDS IT TO MICHAEL'S MOUTH. MICHAEL EATS IT. HIS FACE LIGHTENING NOW.)*

MALC: Want some more? *(GIVES HIM ANOTHER BIT. MALC SITS DOWN BESIDE HIM)*

MALC: *(TO AUD.)* I took another penguin out for myself. I didn't really feel like eating it because the kind of look of Michael in those days put us of eating. Just to be eating with him . . . Rotten waste of a penguin. *(TO MICHAEL)* Got some pop. Want some pop? *(MICHAEL SMILES)*

MALC: *(TO AUD.)* That was a problem. I didn't fancy drinking my pop after him, still. *(OPENS POP. GENTLY HOLDS IT TO MICHAEL'S MOUTH)*

MALC: *(TO AUD.)* We sat for a minute or two. Michael's eyes suddenly turned to the water. I looked where he was looking. This fantastic duck was swimming by us. Bright green head. Michael's face was all lit up. Fantastic. *(TO MICH.)* It's a duck. *(MICHAEL GABBLES SOMETHING)*

MALC: Smashing duck, isn't it? *(TO AUD.)* And we sat a bit more. I gave him another drink.
(TO MICH.) I'm Elvis, Elvis, the King.

(HOLDING HIS GUITAR. MICHAEL'S FACE LIGHTS UP AGAIN ... GABBLES AND MAKES A MOVEMENT WITH HIS HANDS. MALC. PLAYS A CHORD ... ABD ANOTHER. HE HOLDS THE GUITAR WITHIN REACH OF MICHAEL'S FINGERS. HELPS HIM TO PLUCK, MAKES THE SHAPE WITH HIS OWN HANDS AND MICH'S FINGERS PLUCK THE STRINGS IN UNCONTROLLED MOVEMENTS. BUT NEVERTHELESS PRODUCING SOME KIND OF CORD.)

LYNN: *(COMING OUT OF THE TREES)* You playing the guitar, Michael? Aren't you dead clever? *(TO MALC.)* He likes being left on his own a bit, looking at the water. Do you know him?

MALC: I don't know him, no.

LYNN: Gives a drink of your pop.
(MALC. GIVES HER THE BOTTLE)

LYNN: I'm going to be a beautician, amn't I Michael?
(MICHAEL IS NOW WATCHING THE LAKE AGAIN NOT INTERESTED. HE'S SHUT OFF COMPLETELY ... WITH LYNN)

MALC: That's good.

LYNN: Going to a course in South Shields after my year's work experience in this dump. You live here? Never seen you before.

MALC: *(TO AUD.)* I was watching Michael. The minute Lynn turned up he kind of closed up. I mean, it wasn't her, she was dead canny. *(TO LYNN)* I come from Byker.

LYNN: Can you play any Boomtown Rats?

MALC: Just play Elvis.

LYNN: Oh.

MALC: Does Michael like Elvis, you reckon?

LYNN: Know what he likes? Right head case you aren't you Mickey?
(LOOKING IN HIS CHAIR)

LYNN: Where's your tape recorder Mickey?
(FINDS IT. MICHAEL RESPONDS AT THE SIGHT OF HIS RECORDER. SHE SWITCHES IT ON. A VIVALDI CONCERTO)

LYNN:	*(TO MALC.)* That's his scene. Plays that all day, don't you Mickey? Got it from his Dad at Christmas. Some of it's alright but goes on for rotten hours. Come on then, Mickey time we went back to school.
MALC:	*(TO AUD.)* She began to wheel him along the path. Michael was pointing with his eyes at something on the bank.
LYNN:	*(TO MALC.)* Going in for his G.C.E.'s aren't you Mickey, next year?
MALC:	*(TO MIKE)* She doesn't know does she?
LYNN:	What you on about son?
MALC:	He's laughing at you . . . Not see . . .
LYNN:	Got a lot to laugh about *him* . . .
MALC:	*(TO MIKE)* You're laughing because she doesn't know you understand what she's saying, aren't you? *(MICHAEL IS POINTING WITH HIS EYES AT SOMETHING)*
MALC:	He's pointing at something, look at him.
LYNN:	What you on about now Elvis? You do, you can't help it wondering what goes on in their minds. Nowt probably.
MALC:	What is it, Michael?
LYNN:	Ask me . . . you're dafter than him.
MALC:	*(TO AUD.)* I looked down, couldn't see anything at first. Then I saw this flower, like a yellow star in the grass. *(TO MIKE)* It's great. Never seen one before.
LYNN:	Just a rotten buttercup.
MALC:	Is it?
LYNN:	Something like that. Who cares? Come on time to get back to school.
MALC:	You aint nothing but a Hound Dog, Cryin all the time, You aint nothing but a Hound Dog, Crying all the time . . . etc.
MALC:	I've made you some cheese and toast.
MAM:	Listen Malc, I finished with Alex. Last night, do you know?
MALC:	Alright. Yeah, doesn't matter.

MAM:	When you ran off, yesterday. When I came back from work . When I came back and saw your note, Malc. He was in already, sitting there eating a hamn egg pie, not bothered. Like nothing had happened, Ee . . . the fight we had. I threw him out the house.
MALC:	Mam, Can you spare us a quid for Saturday, for bus fare and that?
MAM:	I wish I could do something about my temper. Malc. I wish I could. He was a canny man, Alex wasn't he? Made a lovely father to you.
MALC:	Can I have a quid for Saturday Mam?
MAM:	What for?
MALC:	I told you for the bus and that.
MAM:	I'll give you it when I get my wages, Malc.
MALC:	I'm going to see Michael. He's like a mental cripple, Michael. You know how you get people with body cripple? His brain's crippled. The've a school for them, near Morpeth. Northgate.
MAM:	Poor souls.
MALC:	They're alright, mam, especially Michael. Now him and me are friends.
MAM:	You're not mixing with loonies, are you Malc. that would worry us.
MALC:	I'm telling you, Mam, they're called mentally handicapped.
MAM:	Should I go round to his house, Alex's Malc? After me work. Have a nice day pet. You'd miss him wouldn't you . . . Alex?
MALC:	*(TO AUD.)* Couldn't care less if I never saw him again, but I said, just to please me Mam, Yeah, I would, Mam.
MAM:	I'll go and see him right after me work.
MALC:	You aint nothing but a Hound Dog, crying all the time. *(MICHAEL IS MAKING AN ATTEMPT TO CONTROL HIS HAND AND STRUM THE GUITAR, WHILE MALC MAKES THE CHORD SHAPES.)*

INTERVAL

(MALC CLIMBS ONTO TABLE SINGS JAIL HOUSE ROCK.)

MALC: *(TO AUD.)* I don't know why, couldn't wait to get back and talk to Michael on Saturday. I'm a nut, must be, I mean. Me Mam was out all day Saturday, anyway . . . I suppose . . . and I was sick at playing with the Raby Street kids the same games and the same places . . . or messing about Eldon Shopping Centre, looking at the things I couldn't buy. It was somewhere to go, wasn't it? Got the bus again to Morpeth. Lynn had told us how to find the hospital. She said if I got to the gates about ten o'clock she'd show us where Michael was. Got there just after nine and hung around for rotten hours. No sign of her. I got a bit frightened too, to tell you the truth. People kept walking past us from the hospital real weird like dwarves, and people with twisted faces and everything. I still wasn't used to seeing them like that and they all had to talk to us . . . I mean, it made you feel funny, grown up men carrying teddy bears and women with dolls and toys.

In the end I went over the fields in case anybody saw us, looking for Michael. It was sunny but a bit cold with this wind. But it was nice. The hospital was just a lot of buildings in the middle of fields and trees. If it wasn't for the weird people it would've been dead nice, walking in the grass in the sun.

        You aint nothing but a Hound Dog,
        Cryin all the time,
        You aint nothing but a Hound Dog,
        Crying all the time . . . etc.

I'd got me Elvis gear on and carrying me guitar. Probably everybody thought I was another patient.

I found them in the end, in Carricks Light Bite in Morpeth. Rotten Lynn was scoffing this big cream doughtnut.

LYNN: Look who's here, it's big Elvis!

MALC: *(TO AUD.)* Mike was having a drink of orange, sucking it out of a straw. At first he didn't look at us. I was dead disappointed, and went up to him dead glad to see him.

Hello Michael.

(MICHAEL LOOKING AT HIM BLANKLY)

LYNN: Told you, man. Doesn' know where he is half the time. Do you Mickey?

MALC: Thought you were going to meet us at the end of the road?

LYNN: Was I? Not going to get yourself a coffee or something?

MALC: Yeah.

LYNN: Get me another one, too and a doughnut.

MALC:	Haven't enough money.
LYNN:	Here man, I don't need anybody to pay for us.
MALC:	Want a biscuit, Michael?
LYNN:	Just had one. Don't encourage him to stuff.
MALC:	*(GIVING HIM A CLUB)* I got him a biscuit, anyway and unwrapped it for him. Helped him to eat it He ate it but he still wouldn't speak to me. *(TO MICHAEL)* Got yer tape recorder with you.
LYNN:	Always has. You came all the way from Byker to see him, son?
MALC:	Came in me helicopter.
LYNN:	Great, you give us all a ride back to Northgate.
MALC:	*(TO MIKE)* Fancy going back to that lake, Michael?
LYNN:	We're going along the river. To watch the ducks. Aren't we Mickey. Listen, tell us what's the great thing Mickey has for you? Elvis. What is it then Elvis? Mickey's got, I haven't?
MALC:	*(TO MIKE)* Will I go along the river with you?
LYNN:	Suit yourself.
MALC:	*(TO LYNN)* He's my friend, isn't he Michael?
LYNN:	Not according to Michael, he isn't is he?
	(JAILHOUSE ROCK)
MALC:	*(TO AUD. WHEELING MICHAEL'S CHAIR)*
MALC:	It was dead warm by the time we got to the river. The wind had gone away and the sun was shining and I'd never felt so rotten in my life. Everything had gone wrong that morning, hadn't it? Michael hardly looked at us. Lynn had taken some of the kids who could walk, in a boat, with another nurse. Left me with Michael. She shouldn't, it wasn't allowed, leaving a patient with somebody like me. But that was Lynn.
LYNN:	He'll be alright, man. I fancy going out on a rowing boat. You watch him.
MALC:	I said so...
LYNN:	Mickey, watch us on the boat. I'll wave to you.
MALC:	*(TO AUD.)* I was pushing Michael along the path by the river, and I felt Michael wanting us to stop. I don't know how I felt it. It might have been his gabbling something. I'd been going on at him, moaning away. Came here all the way from Newcastle miles, to see you and you don't even

bother with us. I walked all the way to the hospital from Morpeth and back again, and he stopped us talking, like he'd shouted and made us stop his chair.

(MICHAEL IS STARING AT THE RIVER GABBLING. NOW THAT HE'S ON HIS OWN WITH MALC. HE'S TALKING AGAIN)

MALC: What is it Michael, man? I wish you'd rotten learn to talk properly. I don't understand you, man.

(MICHAEL GABBLES POINTING WITH HIS HEAD AND EYES)

MALC: The boats.

(MICHAEL'S FACE LIGHTS UP)

MALC: You like boats.

(MICHAEL SMILES)

MALC: You want to go on a boat?

(MICHAEL GROWS EXCITED)

MALC: Michael, how can you go on a boat, man? Get you out of your wheelchair into a boat. You can't do it, man.

(MICHAEL'S FACE PUCKERS IN DISAPPOINTMENT)

MALC: It's getting from the landing place on to the boat, Michael.

(MICHAEL TURNS AWAY)

MALC: Look man, If I could do it I would, you know that. It's stupid sulking like that with me. We're supposed to be friends aren't we? If you don't want to be friends, alright, forget...I'll get the bus back to Newcastle.

(MICHAEL HAS TURNED TO HIM NOW, GENUINELY BABBLING AGAIN)

MALC: Yeah, alright, I wish I could get a boat for you Michael, you know that. Two of us on that lake, that would be great wouldn't it? In a great summer day, eh? On a boat on that lake.

(MICHAEL'S FACE REALLY LIGHTS UP)

MALC: There's Lynn, wave to her.

(TAKES MICHAEL'S HAND AND MAKES IT WAVE. MICHAEL LAUGHS)

MALC: We'll race her will we? Come on.

(HE TAKES THE CHAIR AND RACES THE BOAT)

MALC: Beat her, by miles.

(MICHAEL IS STILL LAUGHING WITH HIS EYES)

MALC: *(SHOUTING)* Beat you, beat you, beat you.

(HOLDING UP MICHAEL'S HAND)

MALC: The winner!

(JAILHOUSE ROCK)

JACKIE:	That's a good job that. You want to put a cripple on a boat, in the sea?
MALC:	On a lake, and he's a mental cripple, Jackie.
JACKIE:	That's right, he's a cripple. Put him on a boat.
MALC:	You going to do it?
JACKIE:	Can it be done? I don't know if it can be done, do I? That's what's to be found out.
MALC:	*(TO AUD.)* Should've seen the carry on getting his basket of pigeons on the bus. Fighting with everybody. I didn't know who else to ask, but... did I? I mean, Jackie was supposed to be one of the best joiners in Newcastle before he retired.
JACKIE:	Hold the tape firm, man. It's wide enough to get his chair right on the jetty. Yes it would be. *(MAKING A NOTE OF MEASUREMENTS)*
MALC:	You reckon you can make something to get him on the boat?
JACKIE:	Finding our, amn't I? *(LOOKING OUT AT LAKE.)*
JACKIE:	Canny lake. Have to get strong posts up to here, to sling him on to the boat, clear of his chair. What's he weigh, then? Need his weight to work out how strong to make it.
MALC:	Be heavy.
JACKIE:	What's his weight, man?
MALC:	Have to find out, won't I?
LYNN:	How do I know what weight he is, man?
JACKIE:	I mean, if you haven't the weight you're working blind, aren't you?
LYNN:	Who's he?
MALC:	*(TO AUD.)* We'd got to the hospital, to ask Lynn.
JACKIE:	You a nurse?
MALC:	She's going to be a beautician.
LYNN:	What's in there? *(POINTING TO THE BASKET)*
JACKIE:	The wife was a hairdresser, Shields Road.
LYNN:	*(INTERESTED)* Is she?
JACKIE:	Dead now.
LYNN:	That's a shame.

MALC:	Look, you can find out somewhere how much he weighs can't you?
LYNN:	Did she own her own shop, and that?
JACKIE:	Pigeons, in the basket.
LYNN:	Oh.
JACKIE:	See I need to know what weight we're handling for the framework.
LYNN:	He's not got *you* in this, has he?
MALC:	Michael wants to go on a boat, Lynn, I'm telling you.
LYNN:	Rotten drown him, in the end, that's what ye're gonna do.
MALC:	*(TO AUD.)* Michael was outside. He must have heard us talking, he started crying for us.
LYNN:	*(GOING TO HIM)* What's the matter, now.
MALC:	I was just coming, Michael, man. This is Jackie, he's going to get you on a boat.
JACKIE:	I'm making no promises, about... *(GOES TO LIFT HIM)*
LYNN:	Don't touch him. Start him screaming, man. *(JACKIE GOES TO HIM NEVERTHELESS)*
JACKIE:	Solid, if we said about nine to eleven stone. Allow eleven stone.
LYNN:	Look at him, mister. You can see, doesn't even know what a boat is. It's just him there, he's a nut. Can't make up his mind if he's Elvis Presley or Buddy Holly.
JACKIE:	He's Elvis Pelvis no doubt about it.
MALC:	*(TO MICHAEL)* I wish you'd rotten just say one word. Just to show them, Michael. Even if you said my name. Malc. Say Malc. Say Malc. *(MICHAEL STRUGGLES HOPELESSLY)*
MALC:	You're not trying.
LYNN:	Leave him alone, man. You'll start him screaming.
MALC:	Say Malc. Come on, like that Malc. Malc. *(MICHAEL STRUGGLES)*
LYNN:	Look you've got him upset now.
JACKIE:	People get upset man. That's people, isn't it. Listen, son *(TO MICHAEL)* You want to go on a boat on that lake, do you?

LYNN: I'm having nothing to do with it. He'll get drowned in the end, I am rotten telling you.

JACKIE: I've told you I can't make any promises.

LYNN: I'm telling you, rotten Elvis, if you try anything I'll report you, I will.

MALC: Look, man Jackie knows what he's doing.
(MICHAEL IS BABBLING)

MALC: He wants to see inside the basket.

JACKIE: *(TO MIKE)* Want to see the bane of me life do you?
(OPENING IT CAUTIOUSLY BRINGING OUT ONE OF THE PIGEONS)

JACKIE: There you are, Walter. Useless fat lump of skin, bone and feather.
*(HE HOLDS IT UP TO MIKE. MIKE TRIES TO REACH AND)
TRIES TO STROKE THE PIGEON. LYNN WATCHES HIM)*

LYNN: He likes it doesn't he?

SINGS LAWDY MISS CLAWDY.

MALC: I'm going to tell my Mamm, lawd,
I'm gonna tell everybody I'm down,
In misery...
Well now...
Lawdy, lawdy, lawdy Miss Clawdy.

JACKIE: Pull, man. That's a canny beam that,... Pull.

MALC: I'm pulling.
(TO AUD.) See, it was alright, saying we're going to get Michael on a boat. You know how you get all these fantastic ideas like me and Peter were going to learn the morse code and signal from our windows to each other... but I never got farther than C in morse code. Peter got to about F, I think and we both got sick. Same with this rotten Operation Elvis, that's what Lynn was calling it. We'd no money, you see, to buy wood, and anyway the old man was a nut about getting the right wood, so he dragged us all over Newcastle where they were knocking down houses, to pick up bits of wood there.

JACKIE: *(PULLING WOOD CLEAR)* Now, that's a canny bit of wood. That's real, seasoned wood that, see it?

MALC: It's good, Yeah. *(TO AUD.)* Trouble is it was *my* idea, wasn't it? So I had to keep kidding I was as keen on it as Jackie. I think me Mams right, when she calls us sometimes a useless waster, I am.

JACKIE:	Come on, then. Get it on the barrow.
MALC:	Well, so Bye, bye bye, baby girl I won't trouble no more, Goodby, Clawdy etc. *(SONG FILLER)*
JACKIE:	That's not sawing man. Put some spirit in it.
MALC:	I'm no good at sawing, Jackie. I'll go and get you a pasty for dinner, eh?
JACKIE:	You've got to learn to saw, man. Watch, *(VIGOROUSLY SAWING)* See. *(HANDS HIM SAW AGAIN)* *(MALC TAKES IT UP—SAWS)*
MALC:	Like sawing concrete, isn't it.
JACKIE:	That's it, Elvis, see. That's yer sign of good pre-seasoned wood. *(LINK SONG)* *(IN THE MIDDLE JACKIE KNOCKING AT THE DOOR)*
MALC:	*(TO AUD.)* Couldn't even get peace in me own house to watch Swop Shop. Saturday, I sent me Mam to tell Jackie I'd a cold and couldn't go looking for wood with him.
MALC:	*(TO JACKIE)* I've a cold, Jackie.
LYNN:	Let us in man.
MALC:	*(LETTING HIM IN)* I've a cold and a sore throat.
JACKIE:	Don't worry about it.
MALC:	No?
JACKIE:	Put yer coat on and a scarf. One of me mates's found us a lovely bit of timber. Washed up on North Shields beach. Always been a good place for wood.
MALC:	It's raining, Jackie.
JACKIE:	Fresh air, good fresh sea air, best thing for a cold.
MALC:	*(TO AUD.)* End up on this beach, fighting a gale, looking for wood. *(TO JACKIE)* I'm freezing, Jackie.
JACKIE:	Kill all yer germs. There it is, look at it.
MALC:	*(TO AUD.)* Runs up to this lump of old tarry wood... *(TO JACKIE)* We come out all the way just for that.
JACKIE:	That's hundred year old seasoned timber. Pity we've got to saw it up to get it on the road.

MALC: *(TO AUD.)* Took us hours to saw it up small enough to get
             on the road. Then we had to wait till some mates of his
             turned up with a fish wagon, to take us back to Newcastle.
             Serves us right for telling lies, doesn't it? Spent all day
             Sunday coughing and sneezing.

LYNN: What happened to you lately? Mickey was dead upset when
             you didn't come.

MALC: *(SHARPLY)* I didn't say I'd come every rotten week here,
             did I?

LYNN: Rotten did.

MALC: I was bad.

LYNN: Bet you were. All wearing off is it, you and Mickey?

MALC: Michael's my friend. What you on about, I'm here now.

LYNN: What about the great Operation Elvis? When you gonna
             launch Mickey then?

MALC: Lynn man, stop fighting with us.

LYNN: Alright, peace.

MALC: I'm still Michael's friend, I am.

LYNN: I know you are.

MALC: It's just, sometimes... it's a long way to Morpeth and getting
             the bus fare and that...

LYNN: I know.

MALC: *(TO AUD.)* That was part of the reason, part was the last
             time I'd been with Michael, we'd had a fight. I never thought
             I'd ever have a fight with Michael, I mean, if he hadn't have
             been in a chair and been like he was, I could've chinned
             him.
             *(MICHAEL IS PLAYING HIS VIVALDI TAPE, BABBLING TO
             MALC.)*

MALC: Yeah, well, it's alright Michael I like words with music, you
             know?
             *(MICHAEL IS STRETCHING FOR MALC'S GUITAR POINTING
             WITH HIS EYES)*

MALC: I couldn't play that on me guitar, man. I can't play the
             guitar, anyway... I mean a few chords I learned.
             *(MICHAEL IS INSISTENT. MALC TAKES HIS GUITAR,
             SWITCHES OFF CASSETTE.)*

MALC: There's a man in New Orleans
                 Who plays rock'n roll
                 *(MICHAEL BABBLES LOUDER AND LOUDER POINTING
                 WITH HIS EYES TO THE CASSETTE.)*

MALC: I can't play tunes Michael, man. I'm rotten telling you. Listen this is a great song. King Creole.

MALC: *SINGING*
 There's a man in New Orleans
 Who plays rock'n roll
 He's a guitar man
 With a great big soul
 (MICHAEL IS NOW ALMOST SCREAMING. HE IS WAVING HIS ARMS IN A SPASM, CATCHES MALC'S GUITAR AND KNOCKS IT TO THE GROUND.)

MALC: Michael, man!
 (MALC. IS SHOCKED AND FURIOUS. HE PICKS UP THE GUITAR)

MALC: You've rotten chipped it. Look what you've done. You stupid rotten idiot. Look you've chipped it.
 (MICHAEL IS LAUGHING WITH HIS EYES)

MALC: You don't rotten laugh at me, I'm warning you.
 (TO AUD.) A real crack, right at the side. Could've chinned him.

JACKIE: Come on, man. Get into them straps.
 (JACKIE COMES OUT WITH THE FINISHED FRAMEWORK FOR MICHAEL)

JACKIE: Get in I want to see if they're strong enough, man.

MALC: *(TO AUD.)* Jackie's made this kind of harness from an old parachute.
 (TO JACKIE) Reckon that's going to hold up Michael?

JACKIE: Get in man and we'll see. Sit on there.
 (FITS HIM IN HARNESS)

MALC: Is it going to holdup?

 That's what we're going to see aren't we? Look at them mortice joints. Not a nail in it, too. All wooden pins, see them? Come on.

MALC: I'm going man.

JACKIE: Ready?

MALC: I said I'm ready.
 (FOLLOWING DIALOGUE IS FITTED IN AROUND ACTION)

MALC: It's working.

JACKIE: Of course it's working I know what I'm doing, don't I?

MALC: Holding us, alright Jackie it's strong enough.

MALC:	*(TO AUD.)* Shouldn't 've said that. Minute I did *(THE CLIP FAILS TO HOLD AND MALC IS THROWN TO THE GROUND.)*
MALC:	Jackie, man.
JACKIE:	How did that happen?
MALC:	Jackie, help us I think I've broken my leg.
JACKIE:	I don't think you've broken yer leg. Wait a minute, see what's happened the clips not strong enough. You weren't in it properly.
MALC:	*(TO AUD.)* Hadn't broken my leg but I'd a big horrible bruise right down it.
JACKIE:	Out of his chair. *(PUTTING HIM DOWN)*
MALC:	*(TO AUD.)* I scrounged seventy P. off me Mam, that night and went to Morpeth. Couldn't wait to tell Michael. *(RUSHING, RUNNING)*
MALC:	Michael, Michael... *(MICHAEL IS BEING WHEELED AWAY)*
MALC:	Michael, man I'm here. *(WOMAN WHO IS WHEELING HIM TURNS TO MALC. A STRAIGHT FACE.)*
SISTER:	Oh, you're the Elvis we've been hearing all about.
MALC:	I just come to tell Michael.
SISTER:	I'm Sister Patterson, Michael's ward sister. Didn't Lynn tell you I wanted to see you?
MALC:	I've just got everything fixed, Michael, Jackie's done it.
SISTER:	Now, Elvis, I want to talk to you.
MALC:	Just telling Michael...
SISTER:	Now, I think it's very kind of you, the way you've been visiting Michael and talking to him.
MALC:	It's not that man. Michael, I tried it today. *(TO AUD.)* Michael wouldn't speak to us, I mean, he was smiling at us and that, but he didn't speak. That was one reason why I did such a rotten thing to him. But that sister, I mean, the way she talked. She was canny. She sat us down in a seat outside and got us some orange, with ice in it and gave some to Michael, I mean... She was dead nice to Michael, too.

SISTER:	Is that nice, Michael? *(TO MALC.)* Now Elvis, it is really good of you the way you've taken an interest in Michael. I'm sure you've helped him a lot, having somebody who visits him regularly like this, but Lynn was telling me something worries me... This idea you have about getting him on a boat.
MALC:	That's what he wants to do, ask him.
SISTER:	Now, I know you want to make him happy and please him but you obviously don't know how dangerous that might be... apart from anything else, lifting him... Michael becomes very rigid, because he's spastic, when you lift him. And if he got any sudden shock like falling in the water.
MALC:	It's great what Jackies made, man. You should see it, it's dead safe.
SISTER:	Now I want you to promise me that you won't have any more silly ideas like trying to get on a boat. Will you promise?
MALC:	That's what he wants man. More than anything else in the world, I know.
SISTER:	Elvis, Michael's been here with us nearly seven years. Every day we've tested Michael and everything else. We know Michael can't talk and understands very little.
MALC:	He talks to me, man.
SISTER:	Are you saying you're cleverer than all the doctors and nurses in the hospital, and Michael's teachers.
MALC:	I don't know.
SISTER:	It's physically impossible for Michael to talk, his muscles won't allow it.
MALC:	He says things to us.
SISTER:	And the extent of his brain damage, we know that he can't even think things like that...I want to go on a boat. I doubt very much if he is even aware of what a boat is.
MALC:	He knows, don't you, Michael. *(MICHAEL CLOSES HIS EYES FOR A MOMENT)*
MALC:	I'll show you.
SISTER:	Never mind that, just now, Elvis. Now will you promise me to forget all about the silly dangerous idea you have of putting him on a boat. *(MICHAEL OPENS HIS EYES, LOOKS AT MALC. WAITING)*
MALC:	Jackie's finished it. it's great.

SISTER:	Will you...because...I'm sorry, if you don't I'm afraid we'll have to stop you visiting the hospital.
MALC:	That's what he wants.
SISTER:	Will you promise, then...
MALC:	*(TO AUD.)* I mean, If Michael would have spoken to us, you know...he just sat there, looking like a rotten dummy, and she was beginning to make *me* think maybe she was right, I was just imagining Michael talking, I'd made it up, like I make up millions of things in my imagination. So I was really rotten to him. I kind of went on her side against Michael.
SISTER:	Promise.
MALC:	yeah, alright.
SISTER:	That's a sensible lad, thank you. That's at least one thing we won't need to worry about, now...Do you want to talk to him before it's time for him to go in.
MALC:	Yeah, I'll talk to him.
SISTER:	It's good for him, children like you coming to see him. I wish there were more children coming from ordinary schools to visit the children here. *(GOING)*
MALC:	*(TO MICHAEL)* Michael, I got a book on how to play the guitar so I could learn to play some of the tunes you like. *(MICHAEL IGNORES HIM)*
MALC:	It's called a TUNE A DAY. It's good I'm going to learn to read music and everything. Alex says he's going to pay for lessons for us. *(MICHAEL STILL IGNORES HIM)*
MALC:	Will I wheel you round for a bit. *(NOTHING)* *(MICHAEL IGNORES HIM)*
MALC:	Look, man, she's right. Don't want to get you rotten drowned. *(NO RESPONSE)*
MALC:	You going to speak to us? Look if you don't speak to us I might as well go home. I came out tonight especially to tell you, Michael, man I *couldn't help it* I mean, she's a sister and everything. *(MICHAEL HAS LOST HIS GRIP OF HIS CASSETE IT DROPS TO THE GROUND)*

MALC:	*(TO AUD.)* I picked it up and put it back on his chair, and then, he opened his eyes to us, could see he was hating us. *(TO MICHAEL)* There's yer cassette, man. *(MICHAEL DELIBERATELY WITH ALL HIS STRENGTH SPITS IN MALC'S FACE)*
MALC:	Filthy rotten pig! *(WIPING THE SPITTLE FROM FACE. MICHAEL IS BABBLING IN REAL ANGER)*
MALC:	Rotten come here all the way to see you. *(GRIPPING HIM)*
MALC:	Could rotten chin you, deserve it, rotten filthy dirty pig. *(SHAKING HIM)*
MALC:	*(TO AUD.)* Could've rotten murdered him. That temper I've got. In the end I kind of stopped myself. I let go of him and started to go off without speaking to him. Rotten hating him.
MALC:	*(SHOUTING)* Rotten stupid filthy cripple. I just turned away, going off. Sock! Then I remembered I'd left the stupid brake off his stupid chair and I didn't want it to start rolling down the hill, or anything. I went back to him, and he was just sitting there, not making any noise...but down his cheek, two tears were going down. From his eyes. I'd never had that feeling before... looking at him, and there were two tears running down his face. *(TO MICHAEL)* What's the matter, Michael? I didn't hurt you man. What you crying for man? *(TO AUD.)* I wiped the tears off his face with my hand and two more rotten tears came. *(TO MICHAEL* Stop it man, what you crying for? Stop rotten crying! Look man, I'm sorry, it's just my temper. Me Mam says when I lose me temper, I could kill somebody. I'm sorry. Look, she just got us all mixed up. You're still my friend aren't you man? Come on, I'm still yer friend amn't I? Look I want to go in the boat with you as much as you do, man. *(MICHAEL IS CALM NOW)*
MALC:	Look, listen first day it's hot, right, are you listening. Well Jackie and me'll organise it. Right? Jackie's got a friend with a van. We'll go out on that lake, right? It'll be safe, I mean, you should see what Jackie's made. Lifts us right up in the air. First time we tried it, mind, landed us right on me bum. Still black and blue from that. *(MICHAEL IS SMILING NOW. HE IS MOVING HIS ARMS, TRYING TO CONTROL THEM LOOKING DOWN AT THEM)* *(MALC. TAKES HIS HAND)*

MALC:	Right, we friends, now? (MICHAEL IS SMILING)
MALC:	Mind, you're as bad as me, aren't you. Rotten temper you've got. *(MICHAEL IS LAUGHING WITH HIS EYES NOW)*
MALC:	Well you can burn my house, steal my car, drink my liquor from my old fruit jar, Do anything you want to do, but, ugh huh honey, Lay off my shoes. Don't you step on my blue suede shoes, You can do anything but lay off my blue suede shoes.
MALC:	Come on, man.
LYNN:	*(WITH MICHAEL)* I'm coming, I'm going to get the sack for this, you know that?
JACKIE:	*(BRINGING IN THE FRAMEWORK)* Get the jail, never mind the sack, stealing a cripple.
MALC:	Not a cripple.
LYNN:	Ee! They wouldn't give us the jail, would they? Listen, we'd better get back.
JACKIE:	Bring him over here, man. Have to put the harness on him. *(TO MICHAEL)* Ready Michael?
MALC:	*(TO AUD.)* It was a fantastic day, just at the end of May. I woke up and I could see the sun was right up. Jackie got a hold of the van from this old mate of his, and Operation Elvis was on. Surprised us, Jackie, he wasn't a bad driver. Once he got used to the gears. The whole operation worked great. I phoned Lynn at the school and she got Michael at the top of the road waiting for us.
JACKIE:	Come on, you get on the boat first, man, to steady it for Michael.
LYNN:	Ee! I don't think we should do it. It's not safe.
MALC:	We're doing it now. You're alright Michael? *(MICHAEL'S EYES ARE ON THE BOAT CLEARLY EXCITED)*
MALC:	Look at all them dragon flies, see them, Michael?
JACKIE:	Get in the boat man. *(FOLLOWING DIALOGUE IMPROVISED.)*
LYNN:	It doesn't look safe to me, if anything happens, I'll get it.
JACKIE:	Tested it with twice his weight man.
LYNN:	We wouldn't get prison, would we?
JACKIE:	Not if I don't tell on and you don't tell on me.

JACKIE: *(FASTENING THE HARNESS)* Right, Michael. There we are, me bonnie lad. *(TO LYNN)* Keep him steady.

LYNN: I don't think we should.

JACKIE: Come on man.

MALC: *(TO AUD.)* It was dead hot. The whole lake was shimmering, you know, with the heat on it. And these fantastic yellow and blue dragon flies kept flying over the water, some of them landing on the boat. And the smell of water it was fantastic. Jackie was cranking the handle and Michael was lifted out of his chair. Lynn was holding on to him.

JACKIE: Let go, Lynn, woman.

LYNN: He's going to fall, put him down again.

JACKIE: Let go.
(MICHAEL IS LIFTED CLEAR OF HIS CHAIR, AND JACKIE SLOWLY LOWERS HIM ON TO THE BOAT)

JACKIE: Got him, steady him Elvis.

MALC: I've got him.
(GENTLY MICHAEL IS MANIPULATED ON THE BOAT, SAFETY HARNESS AND BACK SUPPORT FASTENED.)

MALC: Michael, look you're on the boat, man, look.
(MICHAEL IS SMELLING THE AIR, TAKING IN THE SENSATIONS, BABBLING EYES ON THE OARS.)

MALC: Yeah, I'm going, man. You ready?
Jackie give us a push.
(TO AUD.) Jackie gave us a push and we moved right into the middle of the water. It was dead hot. The whole lake was shimmering with the heat on it. And these fantastic yellow and blue dragon flies were flying all over the water. Some of them landing on the boat. You could smell all the flowers from round the lake and water itself. And the boat was moving, just rocking, as we moved. It was fantastic. *(TO MICHAEL)* It's great isn't it?
(TO AUD.) Lynn shouted from the bank.

LYNN: Be careful, man. Watch what you're doing.

MALC: I told you we'd get on the boat together, Michael didn't I? I told you.

JACKIE: Worked like a dream, see it.

MALC: *(TO AUD.)* I stopped rowing and we just floated over the water. It was great, the two of us on that boat together. Floating through the flowers on the water, with the sun on us. It was the greatest day we'd ever had in our lives, wasn't it Michael?

	(TO AUD.) Then a funny thing happened to us. Lynn shouted to us from the bank.
LYNN:	Come on, Elvis, man. I want a shot too *Elvis!*
MALC:	*(TO AUD.)* And looking at Michael's face, the way he was smiling and everything, like, it was even better than he thought it was going to be. I shouted back to Lynn, I don't know what it was, it suddenly got us, her shouting Elvis at us.
LYNN:	Come on, Elvis, man. give me a shot...
MALC:	I'm *not* Elvis, man... What you shouting Elvis at us for? I'm Malcolm, I'm Malcolm. That's who I am . . . I'm Malcolm, Amn't I Michael? I'm Malcolm.

THE END

The Magic Island

CAST LIST

*First performed on tour in Newcastle, February 1979
with the following cast*

Anne: Anne Orwin.
Mam: Pauline Moriarty.
Dad:
Tidy Man: Max Roberts.
Gateshead Goblin: Dave Whittaker

Directed by Paul Chamberlain
Designed by Phil Bailey

ANNE ENTERS

ANNE: Hullo. I'm Anne. I'm going to tell you my story. But I need you to help me.
The first thing is you have to repeat after me: I promise to help Anne to make a play and do everything she asks me to do.
That's good. Now you're all PLAY PEOPLE. In this first part of the story, you're going to be trees and long grass...
(SHOWS THEM AND EXPLAINS CUES).
Now this is the first pat of the story.
Are you ready to listen to the first part of the story? You've got to answer: Yes. We are ready to listen to the first part of the story... Good.

The First Part of the Story.
'Anne Meets the Goblin'

Before I met the Goblin, everything was all different. I was all alone. I mean I had me Mam and Dad and Ginger the Cat. But we lived in this cottage, on the banks of the mouth of a river... Miles from anywhere... And I used to think I was stupid... You know... I hadn't any brains or anything...
Me Dad went out painting and me Mam was a cleaner.
The summer holidays were really terrible. Being weeks and weeks on me own. That was when I met the Goblin... The first week of the summer holidays... But before I met him. Eee... It was dead boring and lonely...

DAD:	I've got a Living Room and Kitchen to paint next week... And an outside to do...
MAM:	That's good...
DAD:	I hope it doesn't rain... The days I'm outside...
MAM:	I hope not...
ANNE:	mam, can we not go back to Gateshead?... I'm sick of this place... It's horrible...
MAM:	It's a lovely place... Got the river on our doorstep... and a garden...
ANNE:	There's nobody to play with... or speak to... When you and Dad go away all day... It's horrible... I'm just on me own... From morning till night...
DAD:	You've got Ginger...
ANNE:	Lot of good he is, isn't he?... Stupid, fat, lazy cat...
MAM:	You've got the telly...
ANNE:	Can't sit watching telly all day...
MAM:	I'll buy you a comic tomorrow...
ANNE:	Not going to last us long... a comic...
DAD:	What's on the telly tonight?
MAM:	Lovely film... With Frank Sinatra... Von Ryan's Railway...
DAD:	Cannie...
MAM:	They've got this new Flash out... In the office... For cleaning Ron... It's lovely... Gives everything a lovely shine...
DAD:	That's nice...
MAM:	Going to need that roof seen to soon, Ron... The next time it rains...
DAD:	I know... It costs money doesn't it... Going to cost nearly a hundred pounds..
MAM:	I could get extra weekend work...
ANNE:	*(TO AUD.)* Great!... I was going to be left on me own... weekends too... *(TO THEM)* Mam, Dad, what about us?... What am I going to do tomorrow?...

MAM:	It's the first of the summer holidays... and you don't know what to do with yourself... What are you going to be like after a week?
ANNE:	*(TO AUD.)* I'm sick... I'm sick of the whole place... I'm going to run away... To somewhere where there's somebody to play with...
DAD:	Switch the telly on, will you, Anne, that's a good lass...
ANNE:	I'm talking to you, Dad...
DAD:	Play with your dolls, man... or your Teddy or something ... I want to watch this film...
ANNE:	*(TO AUD.)* ...I just grabbed me Teddy... and I ran out... I was mad... *(TO DAD AND MAM)* Nobody bothers about me... I might as well be an orphan... with no Mam and Dad... Or anybody... I might as well be on the rotten moon... All the people I can talk to here...
MAM:	Here's ten p., Anne... go down to the village and buy yourself a comic...
ANNE:	*(TO AUD.)* But I just ran out... Not even listening to them...
ANNE:	And that's how I first met the Goblin... I walked miles and miles along the river... Till I came to nearly the mouth... The tide was just out... It was a bit cold... There was these cliffs... going right down to the beach... The water was salty there... You could see the seaweed was beginning there... Showing you were getting near the sea... And I heard this shout from below... Somebody was stuck on the cliffs...
GOBLIN:	Help... Help... Please help us... Missus... Go on... I'm stuck here... I'll die, I'm cold and I'm hungry... I am... I'm dying...
ANNE:	Wait a minute... I'm trying to get to you You don't look as if you're dying... You're just stuck...
GOBLIN:	Oh... Save me... Save me, little girl... And you will be richly rewarded...
ANNE:	I'm coming... amn't I... *(TO AUD.)* I leaned over the edge of the cliffs... And I stretched out my hand to him... Come on... I don't know why you're stuck, anyway... It's easy enough to climb up here...
GOBLIN:	I was hiding from the dragons... You know how they bark at people... and charge at them... I'm talking about the man-eating dragons..
ANNE:	Dragons... Here...?

GOBLIN:	Be surprised what you can find here... Yesterday I saw a Chambit...
ANNE:	A what?...
GOBLIN:	Yes... There you are... You see...
ANNE:	*(TO AUD.)* I never did find out what a Chambit was... *(TO GOBLIN)* Who are you anyway?..
GOBLIN:	Me?.. I've been here for hundreds of years... At least a week... I've moved in from Gateshead... I'm really a Gateshead Goblin...
ANNE:	I come from Gateshead...
GOBLIN:	I thought you did...
ANNE:	*(TO AUD.)* I mean... I just thought he was kidding us on... He just looked like a funny old man to me... I mean... these days... I didn't believe in Goblins or anything else... did I?... They were just stories in books... He was cannie enough...
GOBLIN:	yes... I've moved in here... There's a lovely cave just down the beach... Lovely and dry and warm... and nobody knows about it... I got me son-in-law to bring all me furniture from me old house... They threw us out of it... You know that... They're going to knock it down... All the houses in Goblin Row...
ANNE:	Goblin Row... I never seen any Goblin Row in Gateshead...
GOBLIN:	I know what it is... You don't believe I'm a goblin... Nobody believes in goblins, nowadays...
ANNE:	I'm not bothered... If you want to kind on you're a goblin... It's up to you, isn't it?...
GOBLIN:	What it is... Is your imagination button' hasn't been pressed...
ANNE:	*(TO AUD.)* And he touched the side of me head... I had this funny feeling... He did begin to look a bit strange, when you looked at him... I thought I heard music... coming from somewhere...
GOBLIN:	Now... I promised you a reward... and a reward you will get, miss... You can come along to me cave and take your pick..
ANNE:	You don't need to give us anything,... Anyway, me Mam always told us... Never to go anywhere with strange men...
GOBLIN:	Never said anything about goblins, did she? *(THEY WALK A BIT)*
ANNE:	You're a bit heavy for a goblin...
GOBLIN:	That's because we're made out of good quality material...

	None of your human rubbish stuff... Good solid Goblin stuff... Best thing to help us along the road is to get them trees up there, to sing us the HELPING YOURSELF ALONG THE ROAD SONG... And we can dance the million miles back to me cave...
ANNE:	Million miles...
	(GOBLIN LEADS THE KIDS AS TREES TO SING THE SONG...)
ANNE:	*(TO AUD.)* The song did make it easier... It was great... I tried stopping it... *(STOPS KIDS)...* To see what happened... *(WALKS HEAVILY... SLOW)...* Then I started it up again... *(THEY MOVE FAST AND LIGHTLY)* *(TO KIDS)* Faster they sang... Faster we went... *(TO GOBLIN)* A million miles... There's not a million miles in the whole of the earth...
GOBLIN:	You wait and see...
ANNE:	*(TO AUD.)* And he started counting out steps...
GOBLIN:	One mile... Two miles... *(TO ANNE)* Every step we take's a mile... A hundred mile...
ANNE:	*(TO AUD.)* We couldn't have walked more than a few minutes when he said...
GOBLIN:	Nine hundred and ninety nine thousand, nine hundred and ninety nine... A Million Miles, five inches...
ANNE:	We haven't walked five minutes...
GOBLIN:	But we had a song... We travelled on the wings of a song...
ANNE:	*(TO AUD.)* Anyway... We were in the middle of some rocks now... The old man—or the Goblin... I wasn't sure which now... guided us through the slippery seaweed... Then he stopped...
GOBLIN:	Just making sure there's dragons around... Or whatsits...
ANNE:	Don't be daft, man... *(TO AUD.)* And he led us over the rocks... Right into a cave I'd never known was there... Going deep into the cliffs... And you should've seen his cave... It was really great... Dead comfortable... Tell you what... Put your finger at the side of your head... And push your Imagination Button... *(WITH NOISE)* Close your eyes... And I'll try and make you see it... ... The Goblin had put a lovely carpet over the floor... To make it nice and cosy... And he had a table... and a chair... And at the corner a bed with a lovely patchwork quilt on it... And he had oil lamps... and an oil stove... There was soup cooking on it... And lots of boxes... He was looking round...

	To see what he was going to give us... You can open your eyes now...
GOBLIN:	What can I give you, now... Something nice....
ANNE:	You don't need to give us anything, man... Honest...
GOBLIN:	No... I promised I would... And I like giving things to people I like... I'm looking for something really magic to give you...
ANNE:	If you'd give us something to make us clever... I wouldn't mind that... I'm just stupid, you know...
GOBLIN:	No you're not...
ANNE:	Should see us at school... Can't do me sums or anything... I don't know *where* Timbuctoo is... If I could be clever...
GOBLIN:	You look clever enough to me...
ANNE:	I'm not man... Can't even do me four times table...
GOBLIN:	We'll need to get to the magic island to do something about that... I can't do anything about cleverness meself... What you do is sail to the magic island... And eat some of the Cleverness berries... That's what I did... Just four or five... Brings out all your cleverness...
ANNE:	That's what I want then... Can we go...
GOBLIN:	Yes... Well... We'll have to wait till the right time... Till you're ready for it... I mean... If you take the berries at the wrong time... Won't do you any good at all... Make you even less clever... Let me see now... What can I give you...
ANNE:	I want to go to the island...
GOBLIN:	Oh.... I'll take you... When you're ready... That's a promise... But I have to give you something just now...
ANNE:	*(TO AUD.)* And he gave us a funny shaped kind of stone... *(TO GOBLIN)* It's just a stone, man... I mean it's a very nice stone...
GOBLIN:	No... But look at it...
ANNE:	I'm looking at it....
GOBLIN:	Turn it that way... It looks like a seal... See?..
ANNE:	*(TO AUD.)* Eee.... It did... Now he'd told us...
GOBLIN:	The other way... It's a face... isn't it?.. Now...what else have I got...
ANNE:	*(TO AUD.)* And he gave us a bit of coloured glass... *(TO GOBLIN)* It's just a bit of glass...
GOBLIN:	Ah... But look at it... Look through it at the sky... It's been polished by the waves...

ANNE: *(TO AUD.)* It was... Lovely... When you looked at the sky through it... All blue... and magic like...

GOBLIN: Do you want some Rabbit soup?.. I think I'll have me tea now...

ANNE: I'd better go home... I've to put the pies in the oven for me Mam and Dad coming back for their tea...

GOBLIN: I'll see you again... And you'll see me again... You like me... You see... And I like you...

ANNE: And when I'm ready... You'll take us... To get the Cleverness berries... You promised...

GOBLIN: Don't nag us, man... I promised, didn't I...

ANNE: *(TO AUD.)* He was just saying that, when a kind of shadow fell over his face... and this funny looking man came over the hill... He didn't look all that frightening to me... But the minute he saw him, the Goblin took my hand and shouted to us:

GOBLIN: Hide... Quick... It's the witchman...

(WITCHMAN ENTERS IN A MORNING SUIT... STRIPED TROUSERS... BRIEF CASE... ROLLED UP UMBRELLA... A TIDY NEAT MAN... MOVES NEATLY AND TIDILY...

WITCHMAN: Mr. Mathieson... I know you're hiding somewhere there... Please come out... All I want to do is take you to a neat, tidy, clean Old People's Home... Mr. Mathieson... Give you a nice warm bath... Give you some nice, clean clothes... *(CHILDREN BECOMES THE WOODS)*

ANNE: *(TO KIDS)* I hid behind these trees here... The Goblin beside us...

WITCHMAN: Will you please come out, Mr. Mathieson... I'd hate to get my nice clean trousers all muddy, coming to look for you... But if I have to... Please... Mr. Mathieson... You're making everything untidy... People must live in houses, Mr. Mathieson... You know that... That's the rules... And old people when they have nowhere to live or nobody to look after them, must live in Old People's Homes... Can you think... If all the old men and women lived in caves all over the countryside... How untidy everything would be... Very well... I'm coming in after you...
             (GOES FORWARD... FINDS ANNE...)

WITCHMAN: Ah... Good afternoon, my dear... Do you live in a house?..

41

ANNE: Yes, sir...

WITCHMAN: Very good... very clever and tidy of you... I can see that you're a very tidy little girl... Now... Did you see a rather scruffy extremely untidy little old man go through the woods...

ANNE: An old man, sir?

WITCHMAN: He's living in some damp, cold, horrible, untidy cave... I've been looking for him for months... To take him to a nice, warm, comfortable place...

ANNE: What if he's happy in his cave, sir...

WITCHMAN: He can't be really happy. He thinks he's happy... But old people are just like children... They don't really know what' best for them... If you do know where he's hiding... For his sake... You must tell me...

ANNE: I haven't seen any old man, sir.

WITCHMAN: You're not lying to me, little girl... It's very untidy lying... Lie are very untidy things... As soon as you tell a lie, the minut it comes out of your mouth, it makes another lie itself... An these two make two other lies... and before you know it, you've millions and millions of lies littering the ground... Now... I will ask you again... Have you seen an old man?..

ANNE: I told you, sir... I haven't... *(TO AUD.)* It wasn't a lie... All I'd seen was a Goblin, wasn't it?...

WITCHMAN: Very well... You'll have to excuse me now... I must go and try and find the poor old soul... One thing... Before I go... Promise me, if you do see that untidy old soul... You'll tell me... Immediately... Promise?..

ANNE: Yes... *(TO AUD.)* I didn't know what to do there... Promising like that...
(TO WITCHMAN) What about Goblins, sir?.. Supposing I se any Goblins...

WITCHMAN: Now... That's very, very untidy of you, girl... Dear me... You must have a very untidy mind... *(HANDING HER A BRUSH)*. Here... Take this... Brush it three times a day... That's the only way to stop things like goblins untidying your mind... As you brush, say a hundred times: There are no such things as Goblins... Repeat after me...

ANNE: There are no such things as Goblins...

WITCHMAN: *(GOING)* Very good...

ANNE: *(AFTER HIM... QUIETLY)* But I've just seen one... And he's my best friend...

END OF THE FIRST PART OF THE STORY

... ANNE COMES FORWARD WITH HER STONES... AND
GLASS...
(... NOTE OTHER ACTOR/ACTRESSES COME OUT WITH TWO
BOXES OF ITEMS FOUND ON SEA SHORE. THESE ARE
SHOWN TO KIDS BY ANNE AND OTHER PERFORMERS
AND TALKED ABOUT BY KIDS)

ANNE: Do you want to have a look at what the Goblin gave us... What do you think of them?... Right... Are you ready to listen to the second part of the story?...

AUDIENCE: Yes... We are ready to listen to the second part of the story...

ANNE: Good... The second part of the story... Anne meets the Dragon.

THE SECOND PART OF THE STORY

ANNE: Of course, me Mam and Da' thought I was making it all up...

DAD: Don't be daft, Anne... There's no such thing as goblins...

MAM: Them pies are a bit cold, Anne, man...

ANNE: I told you mam... I got back late... Because of the Witchman...

MAM: There's no such a thing as witchman... Don't be daft, man...

DAD: If there was such a thing as goblins or witches... You'd have seen them on the telly, wouldn't you?.. I mean... in the days before telly... You could believe in any rubbish... But now... With the telly... There's nowt the telly misses... If it's not on the telly... It's not real...

MAM: Mr. Henderson says if I want... I can work an hour extra... Tuesdays and Thursday nights, Ron... And I'll get nearly a pound an hour...

DAD: Canny...

ANNE: *(TO AUD.)* It was no use... They didn't understand... I tried pushing their imagination button...

DAD: Get off, man... What are you trying to do now... What's on the telly tonight, Marge?..

MAM: Ee... Your favourite, Ron... Benny Hill... And Hawaii Five O's on later... And...

ANNE: Mam... Instead of watching telly tonight... do you not fancy a walk... along the river... There's some great stones along the beach... Look... He gave us those... A present...

DAD:	Eh?...
MAM:	I don't like you bringing in rubbish like that, Anne, man... It teks us all me time to keep the place tidy and go out to work...
ANNE:	Look through them, Mam... The Blue Glass...
DAD:	Throw it out, man... Rubbish like that...
ANNE:	Look at the stone, Dad... It's like a seal...
MAM:	I was thinking... Ron... If we hadn't to spend all that money doing the roof... The bit extra money we're going to get... working late... We could go to Majorca for a week... Did you see it on the telly, last night...
DAD:	Harry Secombe's got a house there... Did you know that?... I've always wanted to see his house... There's a man at work... He went there, last year... Saw Harry Secombe on a deck chair with his wife... He waved to him... The man... And Harry Secombe waved back....
MAM:	Ger'away...
ANNE:	(TO AUD.) The day the Witchman nearly caught us... It was a smashing day... Dead hot... The Goblin was just in his vest... I was going on as usual about getting to the magic island...
ANNE:	If I was clever like you, man... It would be better for you, wouldn't it... Be two of us... clever... I could look after you better...
GOBLIN:	It's not time yet... is it?.. The time is not ripe... To take you to the Magic Island...
ANNE:	I mean... A smashing day like this... What happens... If when it's time for us to go the island... And it's a stormy, horrible day...
GOBLIN:	Won't be...
ANNE:	That's what you say...
GOBLIN:	That's the rule... It's never a stormy day when it's time to go... I mean... It might be... once you're crossing the sea... That's different... Listen... Man... Just enjoy the day, Anne... Enjoy the sun... and the blue sky and everything... Content yourself...
ANNE:	Yes... It's alright for you... You've eaten them Cleverness Berries... I haven't...
GOBLIN:	Listen, man... I woke up with the sun shining... and me back giving us gyp...

ANNE: I'll get you some linament from the chemist...

GOBLIN: Will you listen to us... And I burnt my toast...

ANNE: I like burnt toast...

GOBLIN: I was in a right bad mood, I can tell you... I still am... Now, watch this... Watch what you do...

ANNE: *(TO AUD.)* There was this Blackbird... On the hedge by the river... Kind of looking at us... And the Goblin turned to him... and said:

GOBLIN: Ee... I feel sick of me life this morning, Blackie... *(TO ANNE)* What do you think Blackie says to that?

ANNE: Nowt... Does he...

GOBLIN: *(IN HIGH PITCHED BLACKIE VOICE)*... A lovely, sunny, warm day... And you've nowt te de but mess around the river... with Anne there... And you've plenty of food in your cave... and the sun's warm on yer back... And all me fellow birds are singing... and the fish are rising... and the Dragonflies are buzzing all over the place... Ger'away, ye stupid old groaner-moaner...

ANNE: *(TO AUD.)* And it did... It really seemed as if Blackie was saying all this to him...

GOBLIN: *(IN HIGH PITCHED BLACKIE VOICE)*... Tell you what... Give us a smile...

ANNE: It was one of those days, you see... Everything so nice and sunny and peaceful... and then suddenly... Everything started to go wrong... There was a funny buzzing noise... in the distance... And the old man kind of stiffened...

ANNE: What is it?...

GOBLIN: Dragons... They're just coming down the sandy bit... I can hear them...

ANNE: They sounded a bit like motorbikes to me...

GOBLIN: What do you think, Blackie?...

BLACKIE: Time you did something about these dragons...

GOBLIN: You're right...

ANNE: *(TO AUD.)* He had his spade... he used for digging bait...

GOBLIN: You move these stones... I'll dig... We'll just have time...

ANNE: *(TO AUD.)* And he started to dig like mad...

GOBLIN: See... They come along the sandy bit... A hundred miles an hour... If we dig a deep ditch there... That'll spoil their whole run... That's what they love to do... Just run as fast as they can along a straight stretch... If we dig this ditch... It'll spoil their whole game... and they'll stop coming here... and chasing me... and ruining all the peace and quiet...

ANNE: *(TO AUD.)* I could hear them coming... Louder and louder... They sound a bit like motorbikes... I said to the Goblin: *(TO GOBLIN)* They sound a bit like motorbikes...

GOBLIN: That's what they are... Motor Dragons... Spitting flame and fire and poison smoke...

ANNE: Can they not fly... I mean... Over the ditch... I thought dragons could fly...

GOBLIN: Them's flying dragons... That's a different thing... These are Motor Dragons...Motor Dragons... There's all kinds of dragons... Sea dragons... There's a huge Monster Dragon... that shuts out the sun whenever he flies over... He's called the Concorde Dragon...

ANNE: Is that not a plane?...

GOBLIN: That's right... It's a dragon...

ANNE: *(TO AUD.)* And then they were on top of us... Really spitting flame and fire... and poison smoke... We hid behind the bushes... There was a kind of sudden screaming and squealing... When they came to the ditch...

GOBLIN: Listen to them... The're mad... You see... We've blocked them... Serves them right...

ANNE: *(TO AUD.)* They shouted and roared and screamed... They even tried to get across... But the ditch was too deep... In the end... They turned back... the way back... they way they'd come...

ANNE: *(TO GOBLIN)* Ee... That was really clever... I'd never have thought of that...

GOBLIN: Yes you would... If you know the dragons like I did...

ANNE: I told you, man... I haven't any brains... Like some people I'm not clever...

GOBLIN: We're going to have to do something about that... You thinking you're not clever...

ANNE: I'm not... I know... *(TO AUD.)* And just then... The Witchman came... Over the rocks...

WITCHMAN: Mr. Mathieson... What a lovely day... How are you... Nice to see you... Now... Are you all packed up and ready to go... You should see this lovely home we have for you... All clean and hygenic and tidy... The walls are all painted bright green... And you'll be given a new pair of lovely warm slippers...

GOBLIN: Quick, man...

ANNE: Where can we go?... he's got us trapped...

GOBLIN: Get to the river... Quick...

WITCHMAN: Now... Really... You'd think I wanted to do something horrible to you... Listen to this... I don't know what rubbish you're eating in your secret hideout, Mr. Mathieson... But... listen to this menu for tomorrow... Breakfast: ...Cornflakes... Sausage and tomato... Toast... Lunch... Stewed Liver and onions... Mr. Mathieson... Please it's no use... I'll catch you in the end...

GOBLIN: Listen to me—you boring old Pigface... You'll never get me... I'm telling you...

WITCHMAN: Mr. Mathieson... I'll ignore that insult... All I want to do is help you... Now let's stop all this nonsense...You're trapped... Mr. Mathieson... Mr. Mathieson... You're going to make me lose my temper, Mr. Mathieson, with your stupid, untidy behaviour...
(WAVING HIS UMBRELLA)

ANNE: *(TO AUD.)* I don't know what it was... The witchman was pointing his umbrella at us... And there were seagulls wheeling over us... Really screaming at us... I don't know if it was the Witchman's magic or... But they kept diving at us... Screaming...

GOBLIN: *(TO ANNE)* He's got power... You see... over some of the birds...

ANNE: *(TO GOBLIN)* What are we going to do..? He's got us... They'll kill us... These gulls... Look at their beaks... We'd better give in...

GOBLIN: Press your imagination button, Anne, man... Don't waste your thoughts on thinking about losing... Think about winning... Let's see...

ANNE: *(PRESSES HER IMAGINATION BUTTON)*... Quick take your shoes and socks off and swim away...

WITCHMAN: Mr. Mathieson, you'll catch a cold... And you know how untidy a cold is... Mr. Mathieson...

END OF SECOND PART OF THE STORY

(ANOTHER SHORT DISCUSSION BREAK HERE IN TWO GROUPS WITH ANNE AND OTHER PERFORMERS)

. . . . .A BREAK . . . . .

ANNE: *(TO AUD.)* Now, in the third part of the story... You've got to be the thunder and lighting...
... *CUES THEM...*
... Right... Are you ready to listen to the third part of the story?..

AUDIENCE: Yes... We are ready to listen to the third part of the story.

ANNE: Good... The third part of the story... Anne and the Witch Storm.

THE THIRD PART OF THE STORY

DAD: Them pies are a bit overdone... All dried up...

MAM: Did you leave them too long in the oven...

ANNE: I don't think so, mam...

DAD: Can't get any sense from her these days...

MAM: All them Goblins and Fairies and Witches she keeps seeing...

ANNE: Just one Goblin, mam... and I don't see any fairies... *(TO AUD.)* That was the week I really showed them there was a Goblin.

DAD: I'm going to be working late every night this week...

MAM: Eee... That's good... I'm not going to be in either, the next two nights... Mrs. Foster's asked us if I'll come and help in their house... They're having people to dinner and need somebody to serve... Will you be alright... Anne... On your own...

ANNE: Been on me own before...

MAM: But all night... Mightn't be back till near twelve...

DAD: She's got the telly...

MAM: That's right, she's got the telly...

ANNE: I'm watching the swans...

DAD: What's on tonight, then?

MAM: Swans?... It's going to be a smashing night, tomorrow..... Ron,.. We're going to miss Mike Yarwood...

DAD: Eee... We're not...

MAM: And the Two Ronnies...

ANNE: I'm keeping my eye on the swans... Because they've a nest...
           You see... And the Goblin said I should watch it... In case
           any stupid kid came along and tried to steal the eggs...

DAD: You can tell us some of the jokes in the Two Ronnies when
           we get back, Anne...

ANNE: I told you... I'm not going to watch the telly, Dad... I'm going
           out...

DAD: Do you hear that?.. What's come over you... Never used to
           be able to get you away from the telly...

MAM: *(TO DAD)* I'm going to be wearing one of them proper maid's
           outfits... you know... Ron... To serve the dinner... It's a real
           posh party... *(TO ANNE)* I'll try and bring you back some
           cakes or something nice leftover, Anne...

ANNE: *(TO AUD.)* So that was me... Left on me own... all day till
           nearly midnight... Good job I'd got the Goblin for company...
           and I could even speak to Ginger... But that storm... That
           night of the storm... I was just coming back from watching
           the swans... When suddenly the sky darkened...
           (CUE KIDS TO STORM)
           ... It got darker and darker... And the lightning was flashing
           all over the place... And the wind was growing stronger and
           stronger... Rattling the windows... The rain was coming
           through the celing... Eee... it was horrible... I hid under the
           blankets in me bed... But I was still frightened... I peeped
           out... and the wind was pulling off the roof of the house... I
           could see it... Plaster was falling... and there was a gap... to
           the sky... *(TO HERSELF)* ... The whole house is going to
           come down on top of us...

ANNE: *(TO AUD.)* ... And just as I was saying that... The Goblin was
           there...

GOBLIN: Yer roof's coming off...

ANNE: What are we going to do...

GOBLIN: You know who's doing all this... Don't you?...

ANNE: It's a storm...

GOBLIN: It's a Witch Storm... Look out there...

ANNE: I looked out the window...
           *... THE WITCHMAN IS STANDING... HIS ARMS OUTSTRETCHED
           ... HIS UMBRELLA IN THE AIR...*

ANNE: Did you know... I'd be here on me own... Frightened...

GOBLIN:	That's what imagination's for, too... isn't it... To think about what's happening to people you like... You told us your Mam and Dad were working late... First crack of thunder... I said to myself; Anne's going to be needing me...
ANNE:	but he's going to get you, too, now... Now you're out of your cave.
GOBLIN:	First thing is to stop that roof flying off... Without a roof, we won't have any chance at all... Got any ropes... Heavy stones... Come on... We'd better get out... and fix it...
ANNE:	*(TO AUD.)* He was dead clever... He hammered and banged... and tied ropes with stones... and screws and planks...
GOBLIN:	I'm a joiner Goblin, you know... As well as a Gateshead Goblin...
ANNE:	*(TO AUD.)* We were both soaked to the skin... But the roof was all tied down and safe now... I was just making the Goblin a cup of cocoa to warm him up... When Ginger's hair kind of stood up... and she gave this horrible scream...
GOBLIN:	It's the Witchman... He's coming right here... I didn't think he'd have the nerve to come right here... he doesn't know yer Mam and Dad aren't here...
ANNE:	What are we going to do?... If he finds you here...
GOBLIN:	What am I going to do, Anne, man... You're the clever one...
ANNE:	You know I'm not, man...
GOBLIN:	You'll have to start being clever now... I'm not going to be caught now...
ANNE:	*(TO AUD.)* I couldn't think what to do... I peeped out the window... The witchman was coming closer and closer... And then I had this idea... I threw him me Mam's dress.... and headscarf... and apron... and that... *(ANNE PRESSES HER IMAGINATION BUTTON)* *(TO GOBLIN)* Quick... Put them on... You'll be me Mam...
GOBLIN:	Now, that's what I call using your brains... *(PUTS ON CLOTHES...)*
ANNE:	*(LOOKING OUT WINDOW)* He's coming through the gate... *KNOCK AT DOOR...*
ANNE:	Eee... He's at the door...
GOBLIN:	Let him in, man... *(TO DOOR—IN WOMAN'S VOICE)* ... Is that you, dear?
ANNE:	*(TO AUD.)* I opened the door... and he was standing there... He'd put on his nice mask...

WITCHMAN: Terrible sorry to trouble you... But I'm looking for a friend of your daughter's, Madame...

GOBLIN: Anne's friend...

WITCHMAN: The old man Anne...

ANNE: He's not here...

GOBLIN: Oh... No... He's not here... Never seen him...

WITCHMAN: I saw him around here... He seemed to be working on the roof...

GOBLIN: That was me... I'd put on my husband's old coat...

WITCHMAN: Oh...

GOBLIN: Terrible night... Cup of tea...

WITCHMAN: He hasn't been here, then?... The old man...

GOBLIN: Never seen him...

WITCHMAN: Now... This is a nice tidy place... I can see you're a lady who appreciates tidiness... That old man I'm looking for... He's living in some filthy untidy hideout... he needs help...

ANNE: He doesn't need to be helped... He can help himself.

WITCHMAN: He's very old... He's nearly eighty... He can't...

ANNE: He can... I know...

GOBLIN: Now, now... My dear... Don't argue with the nice gentleman... *(TO WITCHMAN)* I think you're very kind and thoughtful, sir... And if I do see him... I'll give him your message...

WITCHMAN: Never mind giving him a message... Just grab him and keep him here till I come for him...

GOBLIN: Yes... That's a good idea... If I catch him, how can I let you know?

WITCHMAN: If you catch him... Let me know right away... My telephone number is 12345678910...
(GOES)

ANNE: Listen... I feel I'm ready now... To go to the Magic Island... I really do... And get some of those cleverness berries... If it's nice in the morning... Can we go...

GOBLIN: First thing we've got to do in the morning... is get that roof fixed...

ANNE: After the roof...

GOBLIN: *(HOLDING HER FACE... STUDYING IT)* ... Let me see... Hmm... Yes... Uhhu... *Nearly* ready... Not yet, but...

ANNE: I'll never be... You're just saying that...

GOBLIN:	If I say you will be, you will be... I promised... Didn't I... First thing in the morning... We'll have to get that roof fixed...
ANNE:	*(TO AUD.)* And we did... He came the next morning, as soon as me Mam and Dad had gone to work... with his bag of tools... And hammered and nailed and sawed... We worked nearly all the day... he showed me how to measure wood... and saw it and everything... And just before they both came for their tea... It was finished... Better then it had ever been...
DAD:	What's happened here?...
ANNE:	We've fixed the roof... The Goblin's been and fixed it, Dad...
MAM:	Have you put the pies in the oven?..
ANNE:	I put them in...
DAD:	It is, man... Look at it... It been fixed...
MAM:	Eee... it hasn't... Has it?..
DAD:	And whoever's done it, he's done a canny job of it... Look...
MAM:	Eee... It is...
ANNE:	The Goblin did it...
DAD:	Oh Aye...
ANNE:	I'm telling you, Dad...
DAD:	How much did he charge?...
ANNE:	Dad... He just did it...
MAM:	Eee... If he did... Ron...
DAD:	Don't be daft... She's got you believing in Goblins now, man...
ANNE:	*(TO AUD.)* That's the end of that part of the story... Now for the very last bit of the story... We're going to need the sea... and waves... and rocks... and things... and an island. *(ANNE BRIEFS THE KIDS ON SETTING UP THE NEXT SCENE)*
ANNE:	Now... This is the very last part of the story. You've got to be rocks... and the sea... and waves... and wind... *(BRIEFS THEM)...* *(KIDS WERE EXCELLENT AT PROVIDING STORM SOUND EFFECTS)*
ANNE:	Now... Are you ready to listen to the very last part of the story...
AUDIENCE:	We are ready to listen to the very last part of the story...
ANNE:	Right... The very last part of the story... The Day Anne Was Ready To Go To The Magic Island.

THE LAST PART OF THE STORY

ANNE: One morning the Goblin said to us, it's time we started preparing for the day when I was ready to go to the magic island...

GOBLIN: There's only one problem... It's miles and miles across the sea... How are we going to get across...

ANNE: We'll need a boat...

GOBLIN: haven't you a boat...

ANNE: We can't walk across the sea, can we...

GOBLIN: What we going to do, then?..

ANNE: I'm thinking... We'll have to make a boat .. I mean... You're a joiner... and you've got tools... I'll get a book out of the library about making boats... And we'll make one... Will we?

GOBLIN: Right... We'll make a boat...

ANNE: Come on... If we hurry... We can get to the library, now... Before it closes... *(TO AUD.)* Eee... And we did... The two of us... It took us weeks and weeks... We learned all kinds of things about building boats...

GOBLIN: What does it say about bending the planks...

ANNE: *(LOOKING IN BOOK)* You've got to steam the wood...

GOBLIN: Put the kettle on, then..., man...

ANNE: *(TO AUD.)* The Goblin couldn't see very well... So I had to tell him what to do, most of the time...
(TO GOBLIN) You're using the wrong nails... They've got to be copper... Copper nails..

GOBLIN: What difference does it make... Copper or iron, man...

ANNE: The iron would rust away, wouldn't it... In the water... The whole boat would just end up coming to bits... great that... In the middle of the sea... The whole boat coming to bits...

GOBLIN: Alright... Go and get some copper nails...

ANNE: *(TO AUD.)* We were lucky with the sail... During that storm... Somebody had been camping and their tent was torn to bits... The Goblin found a bit of it on the beach... And I cut it and sewed it...

GOBLIN: You're not a very straight sewer... Are you...

ANNE: Doesn't matter... So long as the stitches are strong...
(TO AUD.) And it was all finished... I couldn't believe it...
(TO GOBLIN) It looks just like a real boat, doesn't it?...

ANNE:	You think it'll work?... I mean... If it sinks, the minute we pu it in the water...
GOBLIN:	Son see, won't we... Come on, man... Lift it up... I can't carr it down all on me own...
(TO AUD.) We	
ANNE:	*(TO AUD.)* We pulled it into the water... It was a lovely calm day... Hardly a ripple on the water... It was lovely... *(TO GOBLIN)* Look... Look... It's floating... Look at it... *(TO AUD.)* It looked really lovely... Floating on the calm, black water... The sun shining down on it... It was our boat.. The Goblin was climbing in...
GOBLIN:	Come on, man... We want to try it out don't we...
ANNE:	You not want to try it first?...
GOBLIN:	Come on, man...
ANNE:	*(TO AUD.)* It kind of rolled from side to side for a bit, with m climbing in... But once I sat down... It was great... *(TO GOBLIN)* It's fantastic... isn't it?...
GOBLIN:	Put up the sail... full steam ahead...
ANNE:	*(TO AUD.)* Of course, there was no wind... So we didn't mov very fast...
GOBLIN:	*(TO WIND)* You'll have to do a bit better than that, Wind, man... We're just crawling along here, just now... *(UP KIDS SOUND EFFECTS)*
ANNE:	*(TO AUD.)* And the wind began to blow... The boat just skimmed over the water... it was great... Sailing on that calm smooth water...
GOBLIN:	Over the seas like a bird on the wing... Over the seas to the magic island...
ANNE:	We're not going there today, are we?...
GOBLIN:	No... No... Bit far for the first trip... And you're still not ready yet... but tomorrow we'll go on a fishing trip...
ANNE:	*((TO AUD.)* But in the morning something really happened... That we'd been both frightened of all the time... I'd got up very early... And made sandwiches... and a bottle of orange... for a picnic... It was another smashing day... No clouds or anything... I rushed as fast as I could to the Goblin's cave... Kind of singing to myself... We're going to the Magic Island... I'm going to get some Clever Berries... it's fantastic... I climbec down the cliff, to the cave... And went through the bushes hiding the mouth of the cave... *(SHOUTING)* It's me... I've brought a picnic and everything...

VOICE:	Have you, my dear... That's very kind of you...
	(THE WITCHMAN POPS OUT...)
WITCHMAN:	Mr. Mathieson is just getting everything read... Packing his case... and getting everything all nicely tidied up... Would you like to help...
	(THE GOBLIN IS BUSY PACKING...)
WITCHMAN:	Perhaps you could sweep the floor, de ir...
GOBLIN:	You'd better go home, man... Nothing you can do here now...
WITCHMAN:	Not at all... She can help us get ready for your journey to the Old People's Home...
GOBLIN:	I'm happy here, man... You can see that... Ask her... I love it here...
WITCHMAN:	Now, now, Mr. Mathieson... How can anyone be happy here... Look at these damp walls... And the filthy floor... Are we all ready?.. Let's go...
ANNE:	*(TO AUD.)* He had grabbed the Goblin's hand... Ready to leave... when I suddenly had this idea...
	(TO WITCHMAN) I know... You haven't any power over people who live in a proper house...
WITCHMAN:	I told you that... People who live in proper houses are nice and tidy...
ANNE:	Right then... You can't touch him... He's going to live with us now... In a room in the attic...
WITCHMAN:	A room in the attic?...
GOBLIN:	That's what she said...
WITCHMAN:	Living in her cottage...
GOBLIN:	That's it...
WITCHMAN:	I'm going to follow you... Just in case you're telling me another lie...
ANNE:	*(TO AUD.)* The goblin was kind of reading my mind... And I was reading his... We went to the beach... to where we'd hidden our boat... Suddenly the Goblin shouted:
GOBLIN:	Oh... Me Hat... The wind's blown it off... *(THROWING IT TOWARDS THE BOAT)*... Get me hat...
ANNE:	*(TO AUD.)* And we ran fast as we could for the boat... Jumpin in... and pushing it out into the water...
WITCHMAN:	Really this is very stupid... They're all waiting for you at your nice new home... Mr. Mathieson... you're making everything untidy again...

ANNE:	*(TO AUD.)* Suddenly the sky turned black... the gulls began to scream at us... The sea that had been so smooth one minute was suddenly rough... Great waves rocked us... *(UP SOUND EFFECTS)*
WITCHMAN:	*(SHOUTING)* Mr. Mathieson, come back... Mr. Mathieson, come back...
GOBLIN:	Put up the sail, man... Quick...
ANNE:	*(TO AUD.)* We put up the sail... it was terrible... Sometimes the boat nearly bent right over into the water... And the waves They were like big mountains...
GOBLIN:	*(TO ANNE)* Balance the boat, man... Like I showed you... When it goes to the one side...
ANNE:	Yes I know...
WITCHMAN:	There's a storm coming up... You'll be drowned...
ANNE:	*(TO AUD.)* When we got out into the sea... It was really frightening... I don't know if it was the Witchman... But the rocks seemed to come out of the water... And then the rain came... and that turned to hail... Stinging our faces... it seemed like years we were sailing... Fighting the waves... and the wind... and everything... But suddenly the Goblin was shouting:
GOBLIN:	Look... It's there!... Look, man...
ANNE:	*(TO AUD.)* And the island was in front of us... The minute the boat touched the shingle... The sun came out... And the wind dropped... We both kind of flopped down on the white sandy beach...
GOBLIN:	Haven't had a bit to eat since that rotten Witchman pulled us out of me bed, this morning...
ANNE:	I've got a flask... and ham sandwiches and everything...
GOBLIN:	Well... So you should have... If you come on an expedition like this... Lets have breakfast then...
ANNE:	*(TO AUD.)* It was lovely... Sitting on the white sands, warm with the sun... Having our picnic... And we were on the Magic Island at last...
ANNE:	Can we get some berries now... Cleverness Berries...
GOBLIN:	I'm forgetting... Yes... Right away...
ANNE:	*(TO AUD.)* We walked over to some bushes...
GOBLIN:	That's right... That's the bushes...
ANNE:	*(TO AUD.)* But there were no berries there...

GOBLIN:	*(SEARCHING)* ... Now... Let's see... There should be some here...
ANNE:	*(TO AUD.)* There were some shrivelled up, withered berries... All black and horrible... But no fresh berries...
GOBLIN:	Wait a minute, now... I've lost track of the date... This is what... July?...
ANNE:	It's August, man...
GOBLIN:	Is it August... It isn't...
ANNE:	It is...
GOBLIN:	Oh... August, is it... That's why there's no berries then... They've all been eaten up by the birds... They come out in July...
ANNE:	You mean... There's no berries at all... In the whole island...
GOBLIN:	I lost track of the dates... You see...
ANNE:	*(TO AUD.)* I'd never felt so miserable and disappointed in me whole life... I'd been looking forward so much to eating these berries... and what they'd do to us... Make us clever and everything... *(STARTING TO CRY)* *(TO GOBLIN)* You mean, we've gone to all that bother... Building the boat... Going through that storm... and rocks... and everything... For nothing...
GOBLIN:	Don't cry, man... Eee... I can't stand people crying... You'll start making me cry, now... I mean... You should never make goblins cry, man...
ANNE:	I can't help it... Now... I'll never be clever...
GOBLIN:	Listen... What are you talking about... What are you crying for... *(TO HIMSELF)* Stop it, man... Stop crying... will you... *(TO HIMSELF* I can't help it... *(TO HIMSELF)* Well stop it... Now... *(SLAPPING HIMSELF)*
ANNE:	What are you doing...
GOBLIN:	I'm telling myself off, amn't I... *(TO HIMSELF)*... I got her into all that trouble... didn't I... Making boats... Coming through the storm... And there's no berries... *(TO HIMSELF)* You were running away from the flaming witchman, you idiot... weren't you... *(TO HIMSELF)* That's right... *(TO HIMSELF)* So what are you talking about... building the boat for nothing... If you hadn't the boat, he'd have caught you... wouldn't he...

ANNE:	I wish you'd stop talking to yourself, man... I really wish you would...
GOBLIN:	It's the best thing at times... To sort yourself out... *(TO HIMSELF)* What about the berries... and Anne wanting to be clever... *(TO HIMSELF)* What are you talking about... Her wanting to be clever?... What about building that boat... Learning to build it... All the measuring she had to do... And learning to sail it... And the way she tricked the Witchman... Twice... Didn't she?.. She's been clever all along... All it was, was she didn't realise it... That's all... That's as good as finding Cleverness berries... isn't it... Finding out you really have cleverness in you...
ANNE:	He's right, isn't he?...
GOBLIN:	Who?...
ANNE:	The man you're talking to...
GOBLIN:	That's me...
ANNE:	You're right... When I think about it... You're right... *(TO AUD.)* ... I was lying on the warm sand... Dead tired... But really pleased with myself... *(TO GOBLIN)* I must have some brains, mustn't I... *(TO AUD.)* ... And the minute I said that... I don't know what happened... I seemed to be spinning round and round... An there was this funny music... It was like I was flying through the air... And when it all stopped, I was sitting on the river bank beside our house... And there was no sign of the Goblin... or our boat... or the island... Me Mam was coming back from her work...
MAM:	Where are you going now, Anne, man... Have you put the pies on...
ANNE:	I've lost the Goblin... I've got to find him...
MAM:	Are you still with these stupid fairies?...
ANNE:	I keep telling you... He's a goblin... Not a fairy...
MAM:	Have you put the pies on...
ANNE:	*(TO AUD.)* I ran to the cave... It was just as if he'd never been... It was all cleared... The bed, and the table and everything had gone... I was beginning to think I had dreamed all of it up... When I saw, in a kind of crack in the cave, this parcel... It said: FOR ANNE. ... There was some books in it... and this ring... And a letter... The books were all the Goblin's books I really liked... Pictures of all the bird and the flowers... around the river... And I was always tellin

	him what a smashing ring he had... It is, isn't it... The letter didn't say very much... He didn't say the ring was magic... But when I turn it...
GOBLIN'S VOICE:	Hullo Anne... Here's some presents for you... The ring's nice... It might be a bit magic... Try it... I've gone away out of reach of the Witchman... He won't bother you now I'm gone...
ANNE:	Goblin, man... I could stand the Witchman chasing us all the time, so long as you were still with us...
GOBLIN'S VOICE:	Remember this, Anne... I will be your friend always... Don't forget that... And don't forget you've found your cleverness now... Keep pressing your Imagination Button.. A lot of love from the Goblin...
ANNE:	*(TO AUD.)* I keep looking out for him... Almost every day... I go down to the river... Sometimes, I think I see him in our boat... But it's somebody else... But with his ring... It's funny... In a way... I feel he's kind of still with me... When I put my finger on it... I can still hear him... *(GOBLIN'S VOICE SINGING...)*
ANNE:	... Anyway... I amn't... I'm never lonely now... And I've always got plenty of things to stop us getting bored and sick...
MAM:	Anne... Have you put the pies on?...
ANNE:	Yes, Mam...
MAM:	I hope you haven't overdone them...
ANNE:	No...
ANNE:	*(TO AUD.)* I'd better go and help me Mam with the tea... That's my story... Anyway... You were smashing, helping us to tell it... Ta... ra... *(AND REMEMBER KEEP PRESSING YOUR IMAGINATION BUTTONS)*

THE END

The Rainbow Coloured Disco Dancer

CAST LIST

First performed on tour in South Tyneside February 1980 with the following cast.

Carol: Denise Bryson
Mum: Val Maclean
Dad: Tim Healy
Elaine: Pauline Moriarty
Derek:
Doctor: Dave Whittaker
SKINS: Sam Johnson
         George Orwin

Directed by Teddy Kiendl
Designed by Phil Bailey

DANCING ON A RAINBOW

There's a place I go to,
They call it RAINBOW TOWN,
When I'm feeling lonely –
When I'm feeling really down.
Rainbow lights are flashing,
The Rainbow music's loud.
I take all my troubles
And I lose them in the crowd –
I lose them in the crowd.

CHORUS:

Dancing on a rainbow,
Dancing through the night,
Dancing on a rainbow,
Dancing on the rainbow coloured
Rainbow Disco Light.

Story goes, a rainbow.
Fell down from the sky.
People danced around it,
and found out they could fly.
I can hear the music,
Miles from Rainbow Street.
I can see the Rainbow –
I can feel the rainbow beat –
I can feel the rainbow beat.

I go through the doorway,
Rainbows in my eye.
The music takes my body
And lifts me way up high.
There's nothing but the Rainbow,
The music and the beat.
I'm just a colour in a rainbow
High up over Rainbow Street –
High up over Rainbow Street.

CAROL: *(TO THE PEOPLE):* ... It was a great disco, that Saturda afternoon... when everything came crashing down... I wa dead happy in those days.
(UP MUSIC, ELAINE AND CAROL DANCING...)
...Elaine was playing this 'horrible' game... I liked that... Because I had to comfort her. I quite enjoy comforting peopl when I'm in the mood. *(TO ELAINE)* Your teeth are nice.

ELAINE: They stick out, man.

CAROL: They don't. *(TO PEOPLE)* They did.

ELAINE: And me shape's dead scraggy... Like a starved chicken.

CAROL: It isn't. *(TO PEOPLE)* It was a bit.

ELAINE: It is... Is it not.

CAROL: No.

ELAINE: Do I not look too bad.

CAROL: You look nice. *(TO PEOPLE)* She didn't look *horrible.*

ELAINE: Why can't I wear clothes like you... You always look dead right... whatever you wear... I look as if I've been to the secondhand shop round the corner and thrown on the first thing I see there... Ee... I'm horrible.

CAROL: No... You're not...

ELAINE: Good job I've one friend in the world... My dancing's not ba ... is it?

CAROL: Good.

ELAINE: Not as good as you.

CAROL: *(TO PEOPLE):* It was better than Elaine's... But it wasn't all that good in them days. Was it?... *(DANCES)*. See what I mean?

ELAINE: Fancy some pop and crisps?

CAROL: Yeah...
(TO PEOPLE): It was great... You see... Right up to that minute... We went over to get some pop... And this lass stopped me... Lisa... I hated her. She hated me... I don't know why... You just can't stand some people... I never talked to her... But this night she was talking to me...

LISA: You've got a funny kind of dance?

CAROL: Yeah... It's called the 'funny dance'... Good, isn't it. *(TO PEOPLE)*. Best way to deal with characters like her.

LISA: You dance different to anybody else...

62

CAROL:	yeah... Me mam's a Disco Dancer and she taught me *(TO PEOPLE)*. Characters like her have no sense of humour... Have they?
LISA:	She is not?
CAROL:	I'm going to get some pop...
LISA:	So am I... It must be you being a darkie... Makes you dance funny...
CAROL:	*(TO PEOPLE)*... Up till that night... I don't know how it was... I never thought about my skin being any darker than anybody else's... I mean I thought about it a bit... I used to think it was the way I got sun burned... Like the first time I was friends with Elaine... She asked me in the playground...
ELAINE:	Your skin's dead dark, isn't it?
CAROL:	Yeah... It's sun burn...
ELAINE:	In the *winter* time...
CAROL:	It stays...
ELAINE:	Oh...
CAROL:	I think it must be something like that... It's just I have darker skin...
ELAINE:	It's nice... I quite like it... It's better than *my* chalky face... God... I wish I was eighteen and I could put on some rotten make-up.
CAROL:	*(TO PEOPLE)*. And times... in the street... or in the playground... stupid kids shouted at us...
SHOUTS:	Darkie... Darkie... Swinging in the parkie... Wog... Wog... Sitting in the bog...
CAROL:	Stupid things like that...
VOICE:	What you doing out the jungle... Woo...woo...woooo... Watch out... somebody's escaped from the jungle...
CAROL:	*(TO PEOPLE)* Didn't take them seriously... I just shouted back: *(SHOUTING BACK)*. I'll rotten scalp you... Rotten pale-faces... Dig a hole and bury yourself and drop dead into it... Put yourself in a sack and throw it in the Tyne. *(TO PEOPLE)*. Used to think all kinds of things to shout back at them... Never bothered me... It was just the way the sun got my skin... I was as white as anybody else... The skins frightened us, though... Terrified me, them rotten skins! *(SKINS ADVANCE ON HER, MENACING...)*

CAROL:	*(TO PEOPLE).* They didn't shout... I'd just be walking down the street... and they'd kind of come out of the lane or something... Dead quiet...
SKINS:	Where you going, Sambo?
SKIN:	You're walking on a white street, Nig...
SKIN:	Who gave you permission to walk on a *white* street, Darkie...?
CAROL:	Leave me alone, man...
SKIN:	Got any money?
SKIN:	*Cost* Darkies, walking on *white* streets...
SKIN:	Come on... How much have you got...
CAROL:	I'll rotten get you... I'm warning you...
SKIN:	How much have you got...? *(SEARCHING HER POCKET... FINDING MONEY)* seventeen p...
SKIN:	Better have more than that, next time... Not buy you a packet of tabs 17p!
CAROL:	*(TO PEOPLE).* The skins frightened me... Yeah... Rotten terrified me, at times... But I could stand that... You could run away from them and dodge them... But what Lisa told me, that afternoon at the disco... I couldn't stand that... That was the worst thing that ever happened in my life...
LISA:	My Mam says your Mam and Dad aren't your real Mam and Dad...
CAROL:	*(TO PEOPLE).* I started trembling and shaking when she said that... That was the worst thing anybody's ever said to me in my whole life...
LISA:	She says one of them Indian Take Away wogs left you on the doorstep when you were a baby...
CAROL:	Who left *you* on the doorstep like... A Rag and bone man! *(TO PEOPLE).* I didn't know what to say...
LISA:	I'm just rotten telling you...
CAROL:	I'm not interested in a load of rotten, stupid rotten lies...
LISA:	You calling me a liar...
CAROL:	Wouldn't waste my time calling you *anything*...
LISA:	Look at your skin... Anybody knows that... Yer Mam and yer Dad are white... aren't they... Everybody knows that... You're a darkie... Yer Mam and Dad are *not* your real Dad! Look at the funny way you dance...

CAROL: That's right... Me Mam and Dad are the king and queen of Africa... and I'm just staying in Benwell till they get the Palace in Africa all ready for me... *(TO PEOPLE)*. I didn't know what to say to her, really... One thing I wasn't going to do... let her see how much she'd upset me. *(TO LISA)*. And you'd better watch out what you say to me... Me Uncle's a Witch Doctor... and he'll make a spell and do something horrible to you... *(TO PEOPLE)*. That frightened her.

LISA: I was just having a conversation with you, man... I'm not getting at you...

CAROL: Better not... See that bracelet on me... That's a Voodoo bracelet... Anybody I don't like... I just have to touch it...

LISA: Carol, man... I didn't say anything...

CAROL: *(THREATENING TO TOUCH IT)* ... And all kinds of horrible things happen to them...

LISA: I don't believe you... You got it in Woolworths...

CAROL: Will I touch it...? *(TO PEOPLE)*. But she didn't wait... She ran off sharp... That was my day finished... It was horrible... I was so happy a minute before... I hated that rotten pigfaced bitch!

CAROL: *(TO PEOPLE)*. Elaine saw I was upset, the minute we started dancing again... But I couldn't bring myself to come out with it to her till we were going home after the Disco. Elaine got it out of me... I had to share the way I felt with *somebody*... hadn't I... I kind of tried to be sensible about it... I am... I'm a sensible character... I really am...

ELAINE: *Can't* be... How can they not be your *Mam* and *Dad?*...

CAROL: Elaine... *Millions* of people aren't my Mam and Dad... And me Mam and Dad aren't either...

ELAINE: You know what a rotten bitch Lisa Gibson is...

CAROL: Doesn't make the truth any different does it...

ELAINE: You're not a Darkie... You're not...

CAROL: I'm a Darkie... You blind as well as daft!..

ELAINE: They are, man... They *are* your Mam and Dad...

CAROL: Please yourself... I'm going home... *(TO AUD.)* But it hit us... saying that... It wasn't really my home any more...

ELAINE: You coming over in the afternoon...?

CAROL: *(GRIPPING HER)*: You don't tell one other single person this... I'm warning you...

ELAINE: I won't, Carol...

CAROL:	Not even your Mam... I know how you tell your Mam everything... Promise...
ELAINE:	Promise...
CAROL:	Or even the priest... when you go to confession...
ELAINE:	I *might* have to tell the priest... I don't know...
CAROL:	You swear to me... You'll never tell anybody... I'm not going to let you go home till you do...
ELAINE:	Carol, man...
CAROL:	Swear...
ELAINE:	I might have to tell the *priest...*
CAROL:	No.
ELAINE:	If I don't mention any names...
CAROL:	No.
ELAINE:	Alright... I'll commit a mortal sin... If that's what you want.
SKINS:	*(STEP OUT AND BLOCK CAROL AS SHE WALKS AWAY.)*
SKIN:	Hey, Darkie... Where you think you're going...
SKIN:	You haven't paid your money yet, for walking on white streets...
CAROL:	I've two P. That's all I've got. Honest...
SKIN:	That's not good enough... How about that bracelet...
SKIN:	Chattie. *(CAROL BREAKING AWAY FROM THEM...)*
SKIN:	*(SHOUTING AFTER):* Darkie...! Rotten come back... We'll get you...
CAROL:	Drop rotten dead!
SKIN:	Flaming rotten get you for that!
CAROL:	*(TO PEOPLE)* It was terrible going into the house... Dad was dancing to this pop programme on the telly...
MAM:	Good disco, pet?
CAROL:	Yeah...
MAM:	Yer Dad's having his own private disco up here... Stewart, love... Give it up... You can't *dance*, man... You're past it...
DAD:	Anybody can dance... You going to dance with me, Carol...
CAROL:	*(TO PEOPLE):* Ee... I couldn't do that... I could *never* dance with him again... could I...? *(TO DAD):* I'm too tired, Dad...
MAM:	I suppose there's an excuse for him... He's still celebrating this new job he's got...

CAROL:	*(TO PEOPLE):* He got his first job.. with the council... He was a builder and he'd got this contract... Building a wall for the council...
DAD:	Anyway... What's wrong with me dancing...
MAM:	Oh... Is that what you're doing... I thought you had a pain, love... You should tell us... Then we'd know what you're doing... Next time say: I'm dancing. Listen. Stop waving yer arms about a minute. I've got an idea...
DAD:	This wall, I've to build. Carol... Right on the main road. Millions of people'll pass it... Say to themselves; "Look at that great wall. Wonder who made that... I mean look at it... what a wall! I'm going to get the bloke who made that to build my house..."
MAM:	Stewart, listen a minute...
CAROL:	*(TO PEOPLE)*: Watch this. Me Mam's worse than me Dad... Two of them like a pair of kids... You've got to watch them all the time.
MAM:	Instead of us having our tea, here...Let's have it on the beach... We'll all go to Whitley Bay...
CAROL:	*(TO PEOPLE):* See what I mean? *(TO MAM)*: mam, it'll be dark, soon. It's still winter... It's freezing...
DAD:	It's spring, Carol. March is spring, isn't it... *(TO MAM)*: Eah... we'll have a picnic on the beach... Smashing...
CAROL:	It's windy, Dad... It's cold...
MAM:	We'll have to have tea to warm us up. Get a blanket to sit on... Have our tea watching the beach.
DAD:	I'll show you where I'm going to build this wall.
MAM:	Yeah. We're dying to see that.
CAROL:	*(TO PEOPLE):* I couldn't stand it. I just felt out of everything. We weren't a family any more. If they weren't *really* my mam and dad... *(TO MAM):* I'll get the sandwiches, Mam... *(ESCAPING).*
CAROL:	*(TO PEOPLE):* ...Ended up on the freezing cold beach... Sitting on a blanket... Eating our dinner... Stopped snowing...
DAD:	Look at them waves...
MAM:	God... Look at them... *(DAD TAKING OFF SHOES... SOCKS...)*
CAROL:	Dad, man...
MAM:	There's ice, man... Over the sea...

DAD:	Sea temperature doesn't change hardly from summer to winter... Coming in...
MAM:	Just for a minute...
MAM:	You coming in, Carol? Look at them waves... They're lovely... The way the moon's catching them.
CAROL:	I'll watch you... *(TO PEOPLE):* ... I saw what she meant... It was great... The moon on the waves... It did... It kind of made you want to be right in them...
DAD:	*(PADDLING):* My God!... It's *diabolical!* ... Taking me feet off...
MAM:	*(PADDLING WITH HIM HOLDING HER HAND):* I know... It's lovely, isn't it...
CAROL:	Come out, Mam, man... You're getting your coat all wet... with the waves... You're going far too deep.
MAM:	Listen... Somebody *tell* that child... *I'm* the mother in the family... I'm old enough now to look after myself... OH... Look at that... Nearly got me, Stewart...
CAROL:	It was great... sitting at the edge of the sea... Nobody on the beach but us... Drinking hot tea... watching Mam and Dad enjoying themselves... I was looking at them... Thinking to meself: Ee... I know they're kind of daft in a way... But they're lovely... aren't they... And then it came back to me again... watching them... What Lisa had said to me about them... It was like a pain in us... watching them... and thinking they weren't my real Mam and Dad. ... All the way home in the car, I just sat staring out the window... I couldn't stand talking to them... ...When we got home, I rushed into my room and put on a record...
CAROL:	*(TO PEOPLE, AS SHE STARTS RECORD):* ...Now that was the really funny thing about us... Watch this... I put on a record... in my room... That's alright... I START THE COLOURED LIGHTS... That's alright... Then I start dancing... Something weird happens to me. Elaine says I go into a kind of trance... I suppose it's my funny imagination... Once I get into the dancing... *(DANCING NOW):* It's probably the lights... (THE PEOPLE BECOME AWARE OF A RAINBOW COMING DOWN FROM THE CEILING...)* I see this rainbow... Stretching down from the sky... I start climbing up... Up and up... Right above the clouds... It is... It's a fantastic feeling... And at the top... that day... me Mam and Dad were there... Having their dinner...
MAM:	Come on..., then Carol,... Your dinner's getting cold..., pet...

DAD:	Fish and chips...
CAROL:	Great...
MAM:	Fancy going to the pictures, tonight, Carol...
DAD:	Star Trek...
CAROL:	Yeah... *(TO PEOPLE):* It was great... I had this feeling... We were a family... Three of us together... *(DOOR BURST OPEN... TWO SKINS APPEAR)...*
SKIN:	Yer Dad's come for ye.
SKIN:	Downstairs... Coming up for you...
CAROL:	*(TO PEOPLE):* I could see him through the floor... Climbing the stairs... This horrible Indian... It made us shiver... Just the look of him...
SKIN:	*(SHOUTING TO INDIAN):* She's up here, mister...
SKIN:	*(SHOUTING DOWN):* Waiting for you...
SKIN:	Been looking all over for you... yer Dad...
CAROL:	Me Dad's here...
SKIN:	Yer real Dad...
SKIN:	Better get yer case packed...
CAROL:	*(TO PEOPLE):* I could hear him... Climbing the stairs... Getting nearer and nearer... *(SOUND OF FOOTSTEPS ON STAIRS)...*
CAROL:	Dad... Don't let him... Da... *(SHE RUSHES TO PUSH THE DOOR CLOSED)...* Dad...
DAD:	It's no use, Carol, pet... We knew he'd come for you one of these days..., pet... *(STEPS NEARER AND NEARER...)*
CAROL:	Mam...
MAM:	Carol,... We can't help you... He's your Dad... He's a right to take you back any time he wants...
CAROL:	*(TO PEOPLE):* The door began to open... He stood there... Looking into the room... This horrible Indian... And I found this gun in my hand... It was in my hand... I don't know where it came from... Just the look of him... Standing there... That Indian... Smiling at us... I hated him... I hated him... I'd never hated anybody as much as that horrible Indian smiling at me like that... *(SHOOTS... SHOT AFTER SHOT... THE INDIAN COLLAPSES...)*
CAROL:	*(GOING TO MAM):* It's alright, Mam... He'll never get me now... I'll stay with you for ever... He'll never come back to me, now...

CAROL:	*(TO PEOPLE):* The record must've stopped... Because I started to slide down the rainbow... landing on the floor...
MAM:	Carol... Pet... would you go to the shops and get us a loaf of bread, love... and a tin of beans...
CAROL:	*(TO PEOPLE):* ...I looked at her... It was all gone again... The feeling of us being a family and all together... She *couldn't* be my real Mam... Could she?
CAROL:	*(TO PEOPLE):* ...The worst thing was going to bed... I could just about *stand* me Mam kissing me goodnight... But I couldn't face Dad kissing me... just like nothing was changed between us... I kind of tried to slip out to me room... When Dad was in the kitchen...
CAROL:	I'm going to bed, Mam...
MAM:	Yeah... You've had a tiring day, pet... *(KISSING HER)* ... Have a good night, love...
CAROL:	*(TO PEOPLE):* Ee... That was terrible
MAM:	You going to kiss your Dad 'goodnight', Carol...
CAROL:	Yeah... Just going to wash... *(TO PEOPLE):* ... Should known Dad better than that... Ten minutes later... He comes into my room... I have a witch in my room... You know one of them that hangs from a kind of spring... He was always making up things she was supposed to do...
DAD:	Witchie got in a bad temper... Because we didn't take her to Whitley Bay...
CAROL:	Did she..? *(TO PEOPLE):* What was I going to do... I didn't even know what to call him now in me mind... I couldn't call him 'Dad' any more, could I?...
DAD:	She changed the house into a boat... and had us in the middle of a storm for hours... Didn't you... It was terrible...
CAROL:	She's always like that...
DAD:	You should've taken her to the disco...
CAROL:	Yeah...
DAD:	Are you alright, pet?...
CAROL:	Just a bit tired...
DAD:	Let you get to bed, then...
CAROL:	*(TO PEOPLE):* He was going to kiss us... God... I kind of turned my face away... so he just kissed my cheek... He didn't let on he noticed something was wrong...

DAD: Have a good sleep, pet...

CAROL: Goodnight... *(TO PEOPLE):* Just couldn't call him Dad... And
            he gave me a funny look... The way I'd kissed him...
            I heard him talk to Mam about it, next day, just as I was
            going out to school... Mam said it was probably just my age...

SKIN: Oombah... Boombah...

CAROL: Drop dead!

SKIN: *(MENACING... TOWARDS HER):* Don't you rotten cheek us,
            Darkie!

CAROL: Leave us alone, then...

SKIN: Don't *you rotten, flaming rotten tell us what to do...*

SKIN: ... Got any tabs...

CAROL: I don't smoke...

SKIN: Wouldn't want to touch them, anyway, if your filthy Wog
            hands've been on them... How much money you got on
            you...?

CAROL: Got two P... Flaming rotten take it... and drop dead...
            (SHE THROWS THE COIN AT THEM... AND RUNS OFF...)

CAROL: *(TO PEOPLE):* ... Me Dad says things always get worse
            before they get better... That was a good saying... Kept me
            going, that saying... Don't know if it's right for everybody...
            But it was dead right for me it got direr and direr... E... It got
            terrible... I got this thing... I was going darker... Kept looking
            in the mirror every morning I got up... *(LOOKS IN MIRROR)*...
            And when I was out in the town with Elaine...

ELAINE: What do you keep looking in the windows for, man?

CAROL: *(TO PEOPLE):* I could tell *her* that... *(TO ELAINE)*: Do you
            think my skin's getting darker...?

ELAINE: I don't know about your skin... But I'm getting bonier... Look
            at us...

CAROL: You're not... is it?

ELAINE: I'm getting horribler and horribler... Yeaugh... Me...

CAROL: Do you think I'm getting darker...?

ELAINE: Tell you what you are getting... A rotten obsession about your
            being a darkie... You're not...

CAROL: *(TO PEOPLE):* Dead good at words, Elaine... *(TO ELAINE)*:
            I'm not... I'm definitely getting darker...

ELAINE: Carol, man... That's all you think about... Your skin...

CAROL:	I don't, Elaine... *(TO PEOPLE)::* I did... And me Mam and Dac not being me Mam and Dad... Even more... *(TO ELAINE):* Wil we go home and play at Sound of Music...
ELAINE:	Not fancy THE KING AND I, better...
CAROL:	I want to be Maria... *(TO AUD.)* Then I had this thing... Walking along Northumberland Street... This lad was coming towards us...
ELAINE:	Tell you what we've never played at for months... West Side Story...
CAROL:	*(TO PEOPLE):* I'd never ever been like that before in me life...
ELAINE:	Will we?
CAROL:	yeah..?
ELAINE:	Will we play West Side Story...?
CAROL:	*(TO AUD.):* I was terrified he was going to shout DARKIE... o' Wog... Or something... *(LAD COMES NEARER...)*
ELAINE:	I'll be Maria... Can I..? Carol, man... I'm talking to you... *(LAD COMING NEARER AND NEARER...)*
CAROL:	*(TO PEOPLE):* He was looking at me... Dead funny... I was sure he was going to shout something at us... I didn't know what I was going to do... It wasn't *me* I was bothered about.. *I* didn't care what he shouted for me... It was Elaine... I'd rotten die... for her... The way she'd be ashamed to be walking with me... I kept praying: "God, please don't let that Skin say anything to us... God... Please don't let that skin say anything to me." *(LAD COMES CLOSER...)*
ELAINE:	You could play that dancer... You know... In the Dance Hall.. Carol, man...
CAROL:	*(TO PEOPLE): (LAD PASSES... WITHOUT WORD.)* he just went by...Ta... God... That's good... *(TO ELAINE):*
ELAINE:	Carol, man... What's the matter with you... Are we going to play West Side Story or not...?
CAROL:	No... It's too sad... I want to play SOUND OF MUSIC...
ELAINE:	I'll be the Mother Superior...
CAROL:	You ever feel dead glad you've got me for your friend...
ELAINE:	Me?
CAROL:	*Me...* man.

CAROL:	... We could go to Newcastle airport and get coffee there... and be air hostesses waiting for our plane...
ELAINE:	How much have you got?
CAROL:	*Do* you?
ELAINE:	Carol... You're in a dead funny mood, these days... Aren't you?
CAROL:	Yes... I am... Do you feel glad you've got me for a friend... You should be.
ELAINE:	If you say so...
CAROL:	I mean... Getting somebody like me to be your best friend... You're dead lucky...
ELAINE:	So are you...
CAROL:	You reckon... I've got sixty P... Elaine, man... It is... It is getting darker, my skin... isn't it?
ELAINE:	Look... If you're worried about it, Carol, man... look at your birth certificate... That'll tell you who you are, and who your Mam and Dad are and everything...
CAROL:	Should I?...
ELAINE:	Just look at it... Just to get that stupid idea out of yer head and be finished with it...
CAROL:	I don't know where it is...
ELAINE:	Ask yer Mam...
CAROL:	What'll I say I want it for...
ELAINE:	You're the one with imagination, aren't you?... You can make up some story...
CAROL:	*(TO PEOPLE):* Took me *days* before I could push myself to asking her... When I did... she went dead funny...
MAM:	Your *Birth Certificate?*
CAROL:	Just at school, Mam... The teacher was giving us a lesson...
MAM:	Listen, pet... The light nights are started...
CAROL:	*(TO PEOPLE):* Me Mam always went daft when the light nights started...
MAM:	Yer Dad's working late... You know what I'd like to do... I'd like to go on a boat...
CAROL:	A boat...
MAM:	That ferry from North Shields to South Shields... It's lovely... You can smell the sea at North Shields... Are you going out with Elaine, tonight...

CAROL:	I'll come with you, Mam...
MAM:	We could get fish and chips in South Shields... Or a Wimpey... We'll have a night out...
CAROL:	Great, Mam... Could I see me birth certificate, Mam?
MAM:	What kind of lesson would they be giving you at school about birth certificates, pet?
CAROL:	Just... You know... About... How birth certificates... told you about where you were born... and who your Mam and Dad are... and that...
MAM:	You were born in Benwell...
CAROL:	I know...
MAM:	And you know who yer Mam and Dad are... That's all it says in it...
CAROL:	I know...
MAM:	I don't know where it is, for the minute...
CAROL:	*(TO PEOPLE):* That was it, wasn't it... That proved it... You don't lose things like peoples' birth certificates... do you..? She didn't want me to see it... And there's only one reason why she didn't, wasn't there..? I couldn't look at her... I don' think she could look at me...
MAM:	I'll look for it, Carol, for you when I've a spare minute
CAROL:	*(TO PEOPLE):* From that minute... I went really weird... It wa$ terrible I *knew* now... Me Mam had been telling me lies all my life... The way she told a lie about my birth certificate...
CAROL:	*(TO PEOPLE):* The next thing that happened to me... was at the Disco... Lisa started dancing with me and Elaine... That wasn't the funny thing that happened... I mean that was funny enough... The way she kept looking at me bracelet and was dead nice to me.
CAROL:	*(TO PEOPLE):* ...It wasn't my imagination... I mean... I couldn't dance... I couldn't get into the music...
ELAINE:	You alright..?
CAROL:	What do you keep asking me that for..?
ELAINE:	I don't know... Do I?
CAROL:	*(TO PEOPLE):* I just couldn't get the rhythm of the records.. You'd never think you could do that... But I'd forgotten how to rotten dance... I was just... I don't know what it was... I couldn't get myself moving right... It was terrible... I was sweating... Trying to get into the music. *(GOING)...*

ELAINE:	Where are you going, Carol? It's only eight o'clock...
CAROL:	I'm going home... Just... I feel funny... I've got a cold...
ELAINE:	I'll come with you...
CAROL:	You're enjoying yourself... I'll go to bed...
ELAINE:	Are you alright?
CAROL:	I've just got a cold... and a thick head...
ELAINE:	You were alright before...
CAROL:	Yeah... Well I'll probably *die* on the road home... It's alright...
ELAINE:	If you're going to *die* I'd better come home with you... If you're going to kind of *collapse* on the road... It's raining...
CAROL:	Won't bother, if I'm dead... will it? You *stay*, man...
ELAINE:	I'd better come with you...
CAROL:	Doesn't *matter*... *(TO PEOPLE):* We got into one of them *boring* arguments... You know?...
ELAINE:	Do you not want me to come with you..?
CAROL:	Yeah... If you want to...
ELAINE:	If you don't ... Tell me...
CAROL:	I'm teling you...
ELAINE:	You don't want me to come..?
CAROL:	If you're dying to come, Elaine...
ELAINE:	*You're* dying... That's what you say... You look alright to me...
CAROL:	You think I'm a liar...
ELAINE:	No... I'll get me coat...
	(WEST SIDE STORY... DYING SEQUENCE MUSIC...)
CAROL:	*(TO PEOPLE):* We played this game on the road home... Me dying and getting buried in that nice cemetery in Elswick Road... Great laugh all the way back to the house... I almost forgot I was miserable...
ELAINE:	I'll get Abba to sing in the church for you... You dying yet..?
CAROL:	*Nearly*...
ELAINE:	Hodgkin Park's a nice place to die... if it wasn't so dark... and all them funny characters were around...
CAROL:	How about Atkinson Road... Under the lamppost...
ELAINE:	Try it...
	(DIES)
CAROL:	Oh... Oh... Me heart... I'm going... Hold me hand... They got us...

ELAINE:	Denton Burn would be good... Like West Side Story... George Chakiris dying under that bridge...
CAROL:	Scotswood Bridge...
ELAINE:	Tell you a great place... The High Level Bridge...
CAROL:	Too far away...
ELAINE:	This lane's good... Isn't it... *(CLUTCHING HER HEART)*
CAROL:	They've got me..! *(SINGING)*
ELAINE:	There's a place for us, Somewhere... etc...
CAROL:	You've to hold me hand... Ee... We're off our nuts, aren't we...
ELAINE:	That was lovely that... Going in..?
CAROL:	Better...
ELAINE:	How's your cold...
CAROL:	Me cold?... Oh... Me cold... Yeah... It's not bad...
ELAINE:	See you tomorrow... Dead good... In the airport... wasn't it, this afternoon...
CAROL:	Yeah... I *might* be an air hostess. Do you fancy it?
ELAINE:	*You* could be... Me with my face and skin and bones...
CAROL:	What about *my* rotten skin...
ELAINE:	You could be one for Africa...
CAROL:	Could be... Couldn't I..?
CAROL:	*(TO PEOPLE):*Rotten Skins were at the top of the street again... *(SKINS STANDING... MENACING...)*
CAROL:	*(TO PEOPLE):* ...I dodged down the back lane... They saw me... *(STARTS TO RUN... THEY RUN AFTER HER)...* Got to the backdoor. Just before them... That was my one bit of luck... It was open... I ran inside... put the bolt on... *(SKINS BANGING AT DOOR... BEATEN...)*
SKIN:	You wait, Sambo... Till we get you... You rotten flaming wait!
CAROL:	*(TO PEOPLE):* ...Inside the house I had a bit more luck... Everybody was watching Mike Yarwood... I got away with a kiss on the cheek from Dad... Mam was a bit harder...
MAM:	Early, pet, aren't you..?
CAROL:	Got a bit of a cold, Mam... *(TO PEOPLE):* That was a mistake...
MAM:	I'll get you a Disprin...

CAROL:	Just going to bed, Mam...
MAM:	I'll get you a hot drink... and a Disprin, love...
DAD:	You not well, Carol...? Come on... and I'll make you better... Eh...
CAROL:	*(TO PEOPLE):* Couldn't face that... (TO DAD) Going to bed, Dad... *(TO PEOPLE):* All I wanted to do was get into me room and put on a record and run away from myself...
MAM:	We're going to Heaton tomorrow... To see your Dad's wall... It's finished... Did he tell you...
CAROL:	I know, Mam...
MAM:	It's just a wall... But we won't get any peace till we go and see it and tell him what a nice wall it is... I've made you some hot orange, love... with a couple of Disprins in it...
DAD:	Did you have a nice time at the airport, pet..?
CAROL:	Good, Dad... Yeah...
MAM:	I'll come in and see you later... *(KISSING HER)* Make sure you're alright...
CAROL:	*(ON POINT OF TEARS, ESCAPING)...*
MAM:	What's the matter, darling?
CAROL:	It's just me cold, Mam... *(CAROL PUTS ON A RECORD. THE RAINBOW COMES DOWN AND CAROL CLIMBS UP.)*
CAROL:	Dad was waiting for me, at the top...
DAD:	I've made a new door in the house...
MAM:	Ee... it's lovely, Carol, pet... We're going for a picnic...
CAROL:	Mam... It's winter... It's snowing...
DAD:	Not through this new door I've found...
MAM:	We've a garden... and everything... Wait till you see it...
CAROL:	*(TO PEOPLE):*...Dad took me hand... and showed this door in the kitchen... I'd never seen it before...
MAM:	Strawberry tarts... and Cider... You like that, love...
CAROL:	Ee... Yeah... Mam...
DAD:	Wait till you see this, love...
CAROL:	He opened the door... And it was like switching on a light... The light flooded in through the door... And the sound of birds singing... and the scent of flowers...
DAD:	Go on... Go out...

CAROL:	I went through the door... and there was the most beautiful garden you could think of... with a pond... and flowers... and a lawn...
DAD:	What do you think of that...
MAM:	Isn't yer Dad clever to make that door, pet...
CAROL:	Ee... Mam... I never thought there was such a lovely garden outside our house...
DAD:	Look in the pond...
CAROL:	I looked at the pond... There were beautiful goldfish swimming and white lilies... Beautiful white lilies... *(TO MAM)*: It's fantastic Mam... *(SHE'S IN BETWEEN THEM... BOTH HOLDING HER... EMBRACING HER...)* They were cuddling us... The two of them... It was lovely... The way we were so close to each other... When this shadow came over us... Shutting out the sun... *(THE SKINS ADVANCE, WITH THE INDIAN...*
SKINS:	That's her... Waiting for you... Got her now... *(INDIAN STANDS... WAITING FOR CAROL... CAROL BACKS AWAY.)*
SKIN:	Come on... Give yer Dad a cuddle...
SKIN:	Come to take you home...
CAROL:	He's not my Dad... That's my Dad... Ma... Dad... *(...MAM AND DAD MOVE AWAY... KEEPING OUT OF IT...)*
CAROL:	Mam... Mam... Dad...
	(SKINS ADVANCE... PULL HER TO THE INDIAN... *(INDIAN SMILES AT HER... MOVES TOWARDS HER... SKINS HOLD HER... SHE BREAKS AWAY FROM THEM. FINDS HERSELF HOLDING A KNIFE... THE INDIAN CONTINUES TO ADVANCE TOWARDS HER. HE IS JUST ABOUT TO PUT HIS ARMS ROUND HER... CAROL TAKES THE KNIFE... PLUNGES IT INTO HIS HEART... SHE STABS HIM AGAIN AND AGAIN... PUSHING HIM AWAY FROM HER... OUT OF THE GARDEN... TURNS TO HER MOTHER AND FATHER.)*
CAROL:	It's alright, Mam... It's alright, now... It's alright, Dad... We can have our picnic, now... *(DOWN RAINBOW...)*
MAM:	I thought you were going to bed, pet...
CAROL:	Just playing one record, Mam...
MAM:	You haven't drunk your orange or anything... It's gone all cold...

CAROL: I just got lost in the record...

MAM: I'll make you some fresh... Get your pyjamas on... and I'll bring it in... Do you want any supper..., pet? *(BENDING OVER TO KISS HER).*

CAROL: Just my orange, Mam...*(TO PEOPLE):* For a minute I was thinking she was... She was my real Mam... I was still kind of at the top of the Rainbow... Then... I saw her face in the wardrobe mirror... beside mine... *(TURNING HER FACE AWAY FROM MOTHER)*...

MAM: I'll bring you in a Kit Kat... Will I?... In case you get hungry during the night, love...

CAROL: *(TO PEOPLE):* Elaine had the 'flu'. I went straight to her house after school. Her Mam worked in Carricks... So she was all on her own that day... *(TO ELAINE)*: What are we goin to do, then?... *(TO PEOPLE):* She had it all worked out...

ELAINE: Play Boy Friends... We've invited our boyfriends up to the flat for dinner... Go out and get a Tandoori from the Indian Take Away... Me Mam left us money for tea... I'm starving...

CAROL: We'll get fish and chips instead...

ELAINE: You can't give boyfriends fish and chips when you invite them to dinner... And get them a nice bottle of wine...

CAROL: I don't like Indian stuff, man...

ELAINE: Since when...

CAROL: Gone off it...

ELAINE: Just get it for *me*, then...

CAROL: Elaine... It's not good for you spicy food... when you're ill...

ELAINE: I'm *better*...

CAROL: You not fancy a chop suey roll and chips...

ELAINE: Man... We've asked Ralph and Jim up for dinner

CAROL: Thought it was Jack...

ELAINE: Call him Jim Jack... Two names...

CAROL: *(TO THE PEOPLE):* That's how this kid found us standing outside the Indians... I couldn't go in... I'd never been near it since I found out about my Mam and Dad...

KID: That your Dad's shop...

CAROL: What you on about?

KID: The Indian... *(MIMIC INDIAN)*... You wish anything... Curried fish and chips... Very good.

CAROL:	I'm the same as you, man... What you on about... I'm not a rotten flaming Indian... *(TO PEOPLE):* The Indian came to the doorway... looking out into the street... He could've been my Dad... He *couldn't*... He *couldn't* be my Dad... He *could*... Because the kid was saying...'
KID:	Look at him... Same colour as you... isn't he... spitting image of him...
CAROL:	I'll rotten chin you... Warning you... *(TO PEOPLE):* ...But he was right... It was like his colour... *my* colour... And his *face*... *(TO KID):*
CAROL:	*(TO PEOPLE):* I just ran off... I couldn't bear going into that shop... Somebody like him couldn't be my Dad... I mean... I suppose he was alright... He had a bit of a funny smell... That might've been the Indian cooking... But he was Indian... He couldn't be my Dad... Not like me Mam and Dad... or Me... Not like us...
CAROL:	*(TO PEOPLE):* Then it hit me... I *Had* to know... One way or the other... *(GOING)* ...I ran all the way to the house... I couldn't wait to see me Mam... and ask her... She was just bringing out some Ginger Bread Men from the oven...
MAM:	I've made you some ginger bread men, pet...
CAROL:	*(TO PEOPLE):* And it came bursting out of me... I couldn't stop it... *(TO MAM):* Mam... Lisa Graham says you and Dad aren't my real mam and dad... *(TO PEOPLE):* She stood there... Holding the tray of ginger bread men...
CAROL:	That's what she said Mam...
MAM:	People say all kinds of stupid things...
CAROL:	Yeah... Mam... *(TO PEOPLE):* I could see she'd gone pale... I'd never seen her like that before... She was trembling... Her hand was shaking...
MAM:	Will I make you some cocoa to have with your ginger bread men...
CAROL:	Yeah...
MAM:	They've turned out lovely... Haven't they... Cannie... It's a shame to eat them, isn't it...
CAROL:	Yeah...
MAM:	You don't believe a stupid thing like that, love, do you..?

CAROL:	*(TO PEOPLE):* I couldn't answer her... I just couldn't... I could see... She was nearly crying... I'd never seen me Mam crying like that before...
MAM:	Carol... Put yer coat on...
CAROL:	I've got me jacket on, Mam...
MAM:	*(PUTTING ON COAT):* ...Come with me, Carol... A thing like that's got to be put out of yer mind right away...
MIDWIFE:	I know, Mrs. Dunn... How children get funny things in their heads...
MAM:	I hope you don't mind, Mrs. Stewart... I thought the best thing was to let her hear it from the woman who brought her into the world...
CAROL:	*(TO THE PEOPLE):* Me Mam had taken me to this woman in Denton Gardens...
MAM:	Carol... This is the midwife... who brought you into the world.
MIDWIFE:	Ee... She's grown into a bonny lass, hasn't she...
MAM:	She's alright... when she doesn't get daft ideas in her head...
MIDWIFE:	Carol, Pet... You listen to me... I don't know what that stupid Lisa Graham's thinking about... But I brought you into the world... And if anybody knows who yer Mam is... it's me... You just need to look at the two of you... and you can see... can't you... Ye've yer Mam's eyes... Lovely eyes the two of you have... and yer face... the same shape... and everything... And yer hair... You listen to me... pet... Never take any notice of rubbish like that... That's your Mam that... and a good, lovely cannie Mam she is to you...
MAM:	You hear her, Carol...
CAROL:	I hear her...
MIDWIFE:	Couldn't get a better Mam in the whole world... Do you know that, Carol...
CAROL:	I know that. I do... *(TO PEOPLE):* We walked home... I still didn't feel right... I knew now me Mam was me Mam... But she still hadn't said me Dad was me real Dad... Had she?
MAM:	Are you alright, now, pet?...
CAROL:	Yeah...
MAM:	Stupid thing to tell anybody...a thing like that...
CAROL:	Yeah...*(TO PEOPLE):* When me Dad came in... I couldn't talk to him... I went into me room... and put on a record... *(UP DANCING QUEEN...ABBA...)*

CAROL: (TO PEOPLE): This was the funniest thing that ever happene
           to me on the Rainbow...
           (MAM AND DAD WALKING WITH HER...)

           (TO PEOPLE): Me Mam and Dad were walking along with
           me... and there was this Indian Take Away's on top of the
           rainbow.

MAM: Tell you what I fancy... A nice curry... Do you, Stewart...

DAD: I do...

MAM: What do you fancy, Carol...?

CAROL: I fancy curried chicken, Mam...(TO PEOPLE): It was alright...
           I knew... They were really my Mam and Dad... And nothing
           could take me away from them... It was a lovely day... The
           sun was shining... Hot... Summer.

DAD: Let's look at the menu, a minute...

CAROL: While we were standing outside... They came...
           (SKINS CREEP UP... GRAB HER...

SKINS: He's waiting for you... Your father... Get in...

CAROL: You rotten leave me alone... I'm warning you...

SKINS: Come on... Get in... He's got your room all ready and every-
           thing.

CAROL: Mam... They're taking me away...

MAM: We can't help you, pet... It's his right... You're his lass...

CAROL: Dad...
           (DAD TURNS AWAY FROM HER... TO PEOPLE...) The way he
           turned away from me... The sadness in his face... It was
           terrible...
           (TO MAM): Mam... Don't let them take me in... Mam!

MAM: You've got to go to your father, pet... He wants you...

SKIN: Come on!

CAROL: (TO PEOPLE): Pushed me right into the shop... I could smell
           the curry and everything... It was horrible.

SKIN: Come on, man... He's waiting for you...
           (INDIAN IS SMILING...WELCOMING HER...)

SKIN: Got your room ready for you and everything... Get in...

CAROL: I won't... I'm not staying here... I'm going back to my Mam
           and Dad...

SKIN: (PUSHING HER TOWARDS INDIAN) That's yer real Dad... Go
           on...

CAROL: He's not... He's not... I know he's not...

82

SKIN:	He wants to show you yer nice new room... Got it all organised for you... Above the shop...
CAROL:	It's not my room... I'm not staying here...
SKIN:	That's the law, man, You gotta stay with yer father...
CAROL:	*(TO PEOPLE)*: I don't know how it was... I could see me Mam and Dad at the other side of the door... They were standing there... They didn't do anything... Like they were waiting... to see what was going to happen... *(...INDIAN IS WAITING... SMILING... WITH LOVE IN HIS EYES FOR HER...)*
SKIN:	Go on, man... He's waiting for you...
SKIN:	Daddy's nice little girl...
SKIN:	Give yer Dad a kiss, man...
CAROL:	I'm not his little girl... Dad... Mam... *(...MAM AND DAD STAND BEHIND THE DOOR... IMPOTENT...)*
CAROL:	*(TO INDIAN... PLEADING... CRYING)* ... Please... Let me go home... Please... I want to go home... Let me go home to my Mam and Dad... Please... *(TO AUDIENCE):* ...And I found this gun in my hand... I think one of the skins gave me it... I' not sure... The funny thing was... This time... I had the gun in my hand... and I knew all I had to do was shoot him... and the bad dream would be over... But I couldn't... I could see his eyes... The look in his eyes... Like sad... and like he loved us...
SKIN:	Come on... He wants to show you your room...
CAROL:	*(TO PEOPLE)*: ...I couldn't shoot him... I don't know why... *(SHE TURNS ON THE SKINS... FIRES... THE SKINS FALL...)*
CAROL:	*(TO PEOPLE):* I pushed at the door with all my strength... And I broke through it to me Mam and Dad...
MAM:	We've been waiting for you, love...
DAD:	Are you alright, Carol...
CAROL:	I'm alright, Dad...I couldn't shoot the Indian, Dad...
DAD:	That's alright, love...
CAROL:	I don't know why I couldn't shoot him... I'm not frightened of him... I'm not frightened of him, now... I'll never be frightened of him again... Will I...
MAM:	Come on, we'll go back and have our tea... *(...GOING DOWN RAINBOW...)*
DAD:	Carol... It's nearly half past nine... Are you not going to bed, man... Go on get ready... and I'll tell you a story...

CAROL:	*(TO PEOPLE)*: I nearly said... 'Yes, I'd like a story'... Then I looked into his eyes... You could see He was hiding something from us still... I knew he wasn't my real Dad... (*(TO DAD)*: I don't want a story...
DAD:	That's alright then...
CAROL:	I'm too tired...
DAD:	Get washed, then... Go on...
CAROL:	*(TO PEOPLE)*: Ee... I went really off me nut... I did... I didn't know *what* I wanted... Times... I'd be hiding away from me Mam and Dad up in that Rainbow world... For hours and hours... Minute I came back from school... Other times... I'd get in this panic... Me Mam had gone away... and I'd lost her... Once, in the afternoon... I ran out of the playground a play time... Just to make sure my Mam was in the house...
MAM:	What are you doing back at this time, Carol, pet? Are you alright...
CAROL:	We finished early, Mam... There was something wrong with the heating...
MAM:	Oh...
CAROL:	*(TO PEOPLE)*: At nights, sometimes... I'd start getting worried me Mam wasn't there... and just shout for her... Mam... Mam...
MAM:	What's the matter, pet?
CAROL:	I thought I heard a mouse, Mam... *(TO PEOPLE)*: Made up all kinds of excuses... just to make sure she was there...
MAM:	Ee... There isn't... Is there... Will I let Tibby sleep with you tonight...
CAROL:	If you want, Mam...
MAM:	Not that she'll do much good... But mebbes her smell'll put her off...
CAROL:	One Sunday, me Mam was going on a day trip to the Coast with the Jazz Band... I didn't want her to go...
MAM:	What's the matter with you, Carol?
CAROL:	Can I not go, Mam?
MAM:	It's just for Mam's, Carol, man...
CAROL:	I could go, Mam... I'll stand on the bus...
MAM:	Carol, don't be daft, man... What's the matter with you...
CAROL:	*(TO PEOPLE)*: I couldn't keep it in... *(TO MAM)*: I don't want you to go, Mam...

MAM:	Carol... You're daft, pet... What's the matter with you... Your Dad's taking you to the Quayside to buy you something nice...
CAROL:	I know...
MAM:	Come on, pet... You're being silly, aren't you? Why do you not want us to go...
CAROL:	I don't want you to go... I want to go with you... *(STARTS TO CRY... MAM CRIES WITH HER)...*
MAM:	Ee... I don't know what's come over you, love... *(DAD COMES IN...)*
DAD:	What's happened here...
MAM:	Leave her alone a minute, love...
CAROL:	*(TO PEOPLE)*: Then I gave meself shake... Stop acting like a flaming baby, man... Come on... *(TO DAD)*: ...Just acting daft, Dad...
DAD:	You alright?
CAROL:	We going to the Quayside, Dad, then?
MAM:	You sure you're alright, pet?
CAROL:	You have a nice time, Mam... *(TO PEOPLE)*: But I was watching the clock all day... till she came back... And I stayed awake in me bed till I heard her coming in... even though she didn't get back till after eleven...
ELAINE:	You not *going*, now?
CAROL:	I'm *sick* of that disco...
ELAINE:	You haven't been for weeks, Carol...
CAROL:	*You* go, Elaine, man... I'll play me records... ... That's all you've been doing for weeks...
CAROL:	I *like* doing it...
ELAINE:	You *said* you'd go with me...
CAROL:	I've changed me mind...
ELAINE:	Carol... What's wrong with you, man... You never go out with me... You've never been in my house for weeks and weeks...
CAROL:	*(TO PEOPLE)*: I hadn't... I just got stuck in the house... I didn't want to leave me Mam... I was definitely off my nut, then...
ELAINE:	Come on, man... You'll enjoy yourself...
CAROL:	I'm staying here... We can play disco's here, if you want...
ELAINE:	I'm *sick* of playing in your house... That's all we rotten do...

CAROL:	Please yourself...
ELAINE:	Will we just go for a walk in the park...
CAROL:	No...
ELAINE:	Go into town and look at the shop windows...
CAROL:	I've seen them...
ELAINE:	I've got sixty P... We could go and have a coffee in the station... and play at going to London...
CAROL:	I don't want to...
ELAINE:	What do you want to do, then...
CAROL:	I don't want to do anything... I'm happy here...
ELAINE:	You don't rotten look it...
CAROL:	I am... I'm happy here... I would be... if people would stop nagging at me.
ELAINE:	Do you want me to go away?
CAROL:	Please yourself...
ELAINE:	I will... *(STOPS AT DOORWAY)*... Carol... What's the matter with you, man...
CAROL:	I'm alright...
ELAINE:	I want you to come out with me...
CAROL:	I'm alright here...
ELAINE:	Carol... I'm sick of coming round for you and you never coming out with me... I'm *flaming sick!*
CAROL:	Too bad...
ELAINE:	I am... If you don't come out with me, now... I'm not coming back again... I *mean* it...
CAROL:	It's up to you... Isn't it... Please yourself...
ELAINE:	I won't, Carol... I mean it...
CAROL:	It's up to you... Isn't it... Please yourself...
ELAINE:	I won't, Carol... I mean it...
CAROL:	*(TO PEOPLE)*: ...Getting on my nerves... The way she was nagging away at me... *(TO ELAINE)*: Go on, then... Nobody's rotten keeping you here...
ELAINE:	*(GOING)*: I mean that... I'm not coming round to see you again... I'm not... I'm never coming round again... *(ON THE POINT OF TEARS)*...

CAROL:	*(TO PEOPLE)*: I put on a record... and climbed up me Rainbow again... *(UP DANCING QUEEN... ABBA...)*
CAROL:	*(PUTTING ON JACKET)*: I got this new jacket for me birthday. It was lovely... Must've cost me Mam a fortune... They bought it in Fenwicks for me... I think they knew I wasn't right and bought it to cheer me up...
MAM:	Do you like it pet?
CAROL:	Ee, Mam, it's fantastic... It's great...
MAM:	*(TO DAD)*: She looks lovely in it, doesn't she Stan?
DAD:	Telling you... Looks a real smasher in it, you do...
CAROL:	*(TO PEOPLE)*: I felt really great in it... I loved it... It was the best present I ever had... That's what kind of blew everything, that jacket... I was wearing it that Saturday morning... The skins got us...
SKIN:	Hey, Darkie...
CAROL:	*(TO PEOPLE)*: I tried to get back to the house, but they beat me to it... Blocked me...
SKIN:	You'd think she doesn't like us, wouldn't you?
SKIN:	Nuh... Just didn't see us, did you, Darkie?
SKIN:	Cannie gear, there... Nice jacket...
SKIN:	Bit of a cheek, mind, wearing a nice jacket like that, isn't it... Sambo like her...
SKIN:	*(GRABBING CAROL)*: I'm speaking to you, Sambo... What are you doing wearing that Smoothie Jacket...
SKIN:	Suit me... Wouldn't it... Give it to me...
SKIN:	You heard her... Give it to her, Darkie... *(GRABBING IT... IN THE STRUGGLE.. SHE RIPS THE JACKET... THIS IS THE TRIGGER... CAROL GOES WILD... SHE LASHES OUT AT HER ATTACKERS...)*
CAROL:	I'll rotten flaming *kill* you! I'll kill *you*... *(THEY BACK AWAY... SHE'S NOW A WILD ANIMAL... TO BE TERRIFIED OF...)*
SKIN:	It's only a rotten *jacket*...
CAROL:	I'm going to *kill you*!... *(THROWS HERSELF AT A SKIN... THEY BOTH FALL TO GROUND... FOR A MOMENT THE SKIN IS STUNNED BY THE IMPACT OF THE FALL... BLOOD IS COMING FROM A GASH IN HER FACE...)*
SKIN:	You've rotten killed her, you stupid rotten bitch!...
CAROL:	*(TO PEOPLE)*: He was lying there... Dead white... Ee... I hadn't...
SKIN:	*(RUNNING OFF)*: You've rotten killed him, rotten wog bitch!

CAROL:	*(KNEELING DOWN TO EXAMINE SKIN)*: ...I just went wild... Are you alright... *(TO PEOPLE)*: He was breathing, anyway... *(TO SKIN)*: It's just a scratch...
SKIN:	You're flaming rotten mad!
CAROL:	I just went wild... You tore my jacket...
SKIN:	Flaming rotten hell... You've broken my rotten head, man.. You're rotten mad...
CAROL:	You've just got a cut... Here... Hold my handkerchief to it.. Stand up...
SKIN:	My rotten head!
CAROL:	Stand up... See if you can stand up...
SKIN:	Where's Tiger?
CAROL:	Ran off...
SKIN:	Rotten Bastard!
CAROL:	Can you walk...
SKIN:	No thanks to rotten you...
CAROL:	Look... I'll take you to the General... Will I?...
SKIN:	You just rotten buzz off... will you... *(ATTEMPTS TO WALK ON HIS OWN... BUT STAGGERS...)*
CAROL:	Come on, man... I'd better go with you to the General...
SKIN:	Flaming hell... You're rotten off your flaming nut...
CAROL:	*(TO PEOPLE)*: He was dead frightened... All the time we were sitting waiting in the hospital... Didn't speak to me... I waited til he came out from the doctors... To make sure he wasn't going die... I mean... I knew he wasn't... but still... He had a bit o sticking plaster where I'd cut him...
CAROL:	You alright?
SKIN:	You still rotten here? You're off yer nut...
CAROL:	Want me to go home with you...
SKIN:	What's the matter with you, stupid darkie...?
CAROL:	I'd better walk home with you, man... I don't want you to flaming die on the way...
SKIN:	If I had to get stitches in my face... Telling you... I'd rotten skinned you... Alive... Telling you...
CAROL:	We were just passing the Indians... I was having this argumen with her... *(TO SKIN)*: I'm not a darkie... I wish you'd rotten stop calling me a darkie...

SKIN: You rotten flaming are, man... Look at you... You're not white, are you...

CAROL: *(TO PEOPLE)*: Then I said to him *(TO SKIN)*: Anyway... What's wrong with darkies, anyway... They're just people, like you and me... *(TO PEOPLE)*: I believed that... I *did*! The Indian was opening the shop... Ready to start his business... The skin pointed to him...

SKIN: *Look* at him... *Smell* him... Smell that *smell*... *Him*... Same as *me*! *Look* at him... *Smell* him... Look at his *rotten oily skin*... I *hate rotten darkies!*

CAROL: *(TO PEOPLE)*: And it hit us... I felt exactly the same thing about Indians... and black people... He'd got me really mixed up, this time, that skin... I *knew* that... I believed *that*, what I'd said to him... They were just people like me and him but my *feelings* were just the same as his. He spat on the pavement just as he was passing the Indian... Like he was spitting at him...

SKIN: I *hate* them!

CAROL: *(TO THE PEOPLE)*: I just ran away... I had to get to my room... and run to my Rainbow... I ran all the way to my house... The Rainbow was in there... In front of me... I was just going to climb up it... when I stopped myself... Something had changed in me... I looked at the Rainbow... I stood there... looking at it... something was stopping me going up it like I always did... I was saying to myself: God... I've got to pack in imagining stupid things like Rainbows... and everything I make up, up there... It's *stupid*... I've got to pack it all in... imagining things... But it was shining... All the colours were shining... and up at the top... everything always worked out for me, didn't it... Not like down here... No... I've got to stop this stupid imagination thing... Half of me was dying to go up and just lose myself in the rainbow... the other half, pulling us away, saying... You've got to stop losing yourself like that... and just say goodbye to that Rainbow and everybody up there...
I turned my back on it... Then I looked at it again... It was just such a great feeling... climbing up... going right to the top into my own world above the clouds... I couldn't give that up, could I? The rainbow was really shining, now... Dead bright... it was like it was pulling me towards it... I don't know what I did... I kind of pulled myself away... I spoke to it, like it was a person...

CAROL: *(TO RAINBOW)*: I'm going to see me Mam... I'll maybe come up again... I don't know... I might do... I've got to see me Mam... *(BREAKING AWAY... GOING TO MAM)*... *(TO PEOPLE)*: They were in the kitchen... Me Mam and Dad... You could feel there was something not right yet... Dad tried playing one of his games...

... This gingerbread man won't let us eat him... Tell him, Carol, gingerbread men are made to be eaten... He doesn't believe me...

CAROL: *(TO PEOPLE)*: I just went straight to me Mam... *(TO MAM)*: Mam... What about me Dad?... Is me Dad me real *Dad*? How come I've got this coloured skin...

CAROL: *(TO PEOPLE)*: this time she really cried... It was terrible... Dad put his arms round her and tried to comfort her...

DAD: *(TO MAM)*: It's alright, love... Come on... It's alright... Carol... leave us a bit... eh... will you... I'll talk to you in a minute...

CAROL: *(TO PEOPLE)*: It was nearly an hour... till he came into me room...

DAD: ...Carol, love... I want to tell you something. Listen... Years and years ago... *Before* I got engaged to your Mam... She got pregnant to some other man...

CAROL: I didn't say anything... I couldn't...

DAD: Do you understand... love?

CAROL: I understand...

DAD: In a way, love, then... you *could* say I'm not your real Dad... But in a way... that's not important... Not at all... Carol... can you not feel that... I've never felt anything else *but* your Dad... I *am*, man... I've been with your Mam before you were *born,* love... I saw you when you were born... a minute after... Do you understand...

CAROL: Where is he, then?... My real Dad?

DAD: H's away... God knows where he is...

CAROL: Will he never come back and take me away...

DAD: Carol, love... *I'm* your Dad... He's away... That's all finished and done with... He doesn't even know you exist... It's finished that...

CAROL: *(TO PEOPLE)*: He had his arm round us, now... I'd never felt closer to him... Ee... I loved him... I looked at him... and I loved him... I was dead happy... I kissed him... *(TO DAD)*: Dad... I love you... I really do... I love you, Dad...

DAD: Your Mam's a bit worried you might hold it against her... I told her you wouldn't... How would you... Go and see her, Carol, Love...

CAROL:	*(TO PEOPLE)*: Me Mam was sitting at the table... She had a gingerbread man in her hand... Staring at it... Still crying... But quietly... *(RUSHES TO HER... ARMS ROUND HER...)* Mam... I love you, man... You know that... I love you...
MAM:	I know you do, pet... I know that...
CAROL:	*(TO PEOPLE)*: Hugging me... The gingerbread man had got all crumbled... *(TO MAM)*: Mam... The gingerbread man's getting all crumbled... *(UP DANCING ON A RAINBOW...)* *(CAROL DANCING WITH ELAINE...)*
CAROL:	*(TO PEOPLE)*: I had this feeling... I was free... I was really free... I knew what I was, now... somebody special... I felt so free... I even went and picked up Elaine at her house... and ended up at the Disco... And a funny thing happened... I don't know what it was... I just felt great... Really moving with the music... I could dance... Just like I danced up on the rainbow... But this time I was on solid ground...
CAROL:	Elaine... I can dance... Look at us... Elaine... Look at me... I can really dance, now... *(UP MUSIC...)*

THE END

Happy Lies

CAST LIST

First performance was on 16th February 1981 at New Town Junior School, Station Road, Hebburn, with the following cast.

Derek: Dave Whitaker
Kamala: Denise Bryson
Shirley: Pauline Moriarty
Derek's Mam: Anne Orwin
Miss Graham:
Derek's Dad: Brian Hogg
Christian Aid Lecturer:
Priest:

Directed by Teddy Kiendl
Designed by Phil Bailey

DEREK:	*(DICTATING TO SHIRLEY)* Dear Kamala . . . *(TO KAMALA)* This letter is from me, Derek Bates. I am eleven. I'm *nearly* eleven. I live in Jarrow. I am writing to you to tell you I am going to help you. I saw . . .
SHIRLEY:	Nuh!
DEREK:	*(TO SHIRLEY)* What you on about 'nuh'?
SHIRLEY:	Like *what*? What are you going *to do* to help her?
DEREK:	Going to help her.
SHIRLEY:	*How*?
DEREK:	Just flaming write, man: 'I'm going to help you'.
SHIRLEY:	That's rotten... Building up her hopes you're gonna help her when you havn't a clue how... It is, Derek, man...
DEREK:	I have... I know...
SHIRLEY:	You didn't tell *me*... What are you going to do...
DEREK:	She's a cripple, isn't she... Gonna help her to walk... Right?
SHIRLEY:	Derek, man! We're in Jarrow – not flaming Fairyland!
DEREK:	*(TOP OF HIS HEAD)* Going to get her a wheelchair. Right?
SHIRLEY:	yeah... That's a good idea... That's being sensible.
DEREK:	*(TO KAMALA)* I am writing to tell you I am going to get you a wheelchair...
SHIRLEY:	*Nuh!*
DEREK:	What's Nuh, now, man?
SHIRLEY:	Wheelchairs cost a fortune, Derek...
DEREK:	We'll get the money... *I know*...
SHIRLEY:	When we're really sure we can get her a chair and we're not going to disappoint her.
DEREK:	Tell you what... *You* write the flaming letter...
SHIRLEY:	Come on, Derek, man... She's *your* friend... Tell her how you found out about her...
DEREK:	I'm gonna get that wheelchair, Shirley... Telling you...
SHIRLEY:	Alright... *(WAITS FOR HIM TO CONTINUE LETTER)*
DEREK:	*(TO KAMALA)* You see... This man who came from India... who got me writing to you... Came to our school... Mr. Sloan, the headmaster's always bringing in all kinds of funny characters to talk to us. Most of them's dead boring... I mean... It's a change from the lessons... It was one of those

bad days for me... Deadly... You know... I mean... Like... I have deadly days all the time... This was like *super* deadly... So after he'd talked... you see... I hung about, at playtime... to help him...
What I said at the start was a *lie*...

DEREK: Sir, my Dad worked in India, sir...

C. A. MAN: Oh... What did he do in India?

DEREK: Sir... He was a soldier...

(TO KAMALA) Pack of lies... First thing that came into my head... See... I liked him... When he was talking... He was a dead nice bloke... I wanted to talk to him...

C. A. MAN: Were *you* in India with him?

DEREK: Sir, it was before I was born sir...

C. A. MAN: Where was he stationed?

DEREK: Sir, I'm not sure... He used to give part of his wages to the poor people there, sir...

C. A. MAN: That was kind of him... *(ABOUT TO GO)*

DEREK: *(TO KAMALA)* He was just going to go off... I wanted to keep speaking to him... That's how I came out with helping you... I mean... I didn't know who you were... But that was the last poster he gonna roll up... And he was going off... So I kind of had to get moving quick, hadn't I?

DEREK: Sir... That girl there... Sir... I'd like to help her... The one that lives in that slum place...

C. A. MAN: In Korrukupet...

DEREK: That's right, sir... Sir, can I help her...

C. A. MAN: *(LOOKING AT POSTER)* This child here...

DEREK: *(TO KAMALA)* Now... This is the funny thing... I looked at your photograph, then... talking to him... And it looked nice... I mean *you* looked nice... I liked you... I mean... Saying that to him... It was... I was just saying the first thing that came into my head at first... I wanted to help you. But when I looked at the photograph again... I wanted to talk to you... I really did... I really started to want to talk to you... And know about you... That's the *truth*... *(TO MAN)* Sir... What's her name, sir?...

C. A. MAN: I'm sorry. We don't have any names for anyone... We probably should. You're right.

DEREK: Sir... Can you find out her name, sir... If you could find out her name, sir... I want to write her a letter, sir. *(TO KAMALA)* I did... The more I looked at that poster... I wanted to write to

	you... *(TO MAN)* I could write her a letter, sir, and she could write back, sir...
C. A. MAN:	Listen... I'll tell you what... Give me your name and address... We have a contact in Korrukupet... She might be able to find out who that girl is... It could be good for her and you – writing to her... It might start something, mightn't it... Give the people in the posters names...
DEREK:	*(TO KAMALA)* I was watching him, rolling up the poster... Dying for him to give me it... I really wanted it... To put in my bedroom... Started working out how I could nick it... *(TO C.A. MAN)* Sir... If you're going to have a coffee with the headmaster, sir... You're better to leave that here, sir... You're better to leave that here, sir. In the hall, sir... *(DEREK'S WRIST ALARM STARTS TO SOUND)*... Then my flaming alarm started to sound...
C. A. MAN:	What's that?...
DEREK:	It's just my alarm, sir... I set it for five minutes before the end of playtime...
C. A. MAN:	An alarm...
DEREK:	I like to know what time it is, sir... *(TO KAMALA)* I've got a thing, you see, about time... I've got a radio alarm... in my room... and a clock. What I fancy is one of them alarms that make tea and wake you up... They're fantastic...
C. A. MAN:	I'd better go and have a word with your headmaster...
DEREK:	*(TO KAMALA)* Then another thing happened... It came into my head... Why did I need to *nick* it... Why didn't I just ask him straight out... *(TO MAN)* Sir... Could I have that poster, sir?... Of the girl... To put in my room, sir... *(TO KAMALA)* And he gave me it... Straight away... Without any bother...
C. A. MAN:	*(GOING)* Look here... If we find out anything... I'll write to you... Alright?
KAMALA:	*(TO DEREK)* Do you play feasts? I was playing feasts the morning the Jesus Lady came with your letter... My mother told me and my sister a Jesus Lady came to Korrukupet to help the people with money from England... My sister said it was from the Queen of England... The Queen was richer than all the rich men in India... Is she? The Jesus Lady came to our hut...
GRAHAM:	Kamala... Kamala... *(KAMALA HIDES UNDER HER BLANKET, PEEPING OUT. SHE SHE DOESN'T LIKE WHAT SHE SEES)* Is there someone in? Hullo?... It's Miss Graham... From

Madras Community... Can I come in?
(AT THE DOORWAY. PEERING THROUGH THE DARKNESS OF THE HUT.)

Are you there, Kamala? Mr. Jagran said he'd just seen you...
(GOES IN... KAMALA TRIES TO BE VERY STILL UNDER HER BLANKET.)

I've come with a letter for you.
(A BIT IMPATIENTLY NOW.) Kamala... Where *are* you? I have a lot of calls to make this morning.
(KAMALA'S FOOT HAS POKED OUT OF THE BLANKET... GRAHAM MOVES TOWARDS IT...)

Come on... I can see your foot under the blanket, Kamala. What are you doing?
(KAMALA GIVES UP... PRETENDS TO SLOWLY WAKE.)

KAMALA:	Who is there? Is there someone there?... Excuse me... I was sleeping... *SITS UP.* My mother is at work and my sister is at work with her. I am only here.
GRAHAM:	I've a letter for you. You're the girl who can't walk, aren't you?
KAMALA:	I can walk. I walk very well. Excellently.
GRAHAM:	Can you?
KAMALA:	And I have no one to write letters to me. You have the wrong person. Good morning, lady.
GRAHAM:	From England. The letter's from England. *(SHE DELIBERATELY DROPS THE LETTER, TESTING KAMALA.)* I'm sorry. *(WAITS FOR KAMALA TO PICK IT UP.)* Can't you pick it up?
KAMALA:	I am not expecting any government letters. From government people.
GRAHAM:	I'm from Madras Community, Kamala... I am not a government woman. Can't you pick it up? *(KAMALA STRETCHES TO REACH IT.)*
GRAHAM:	Kamala... You can't walk. I know... I've been told...
KAMALA:	I have a swelling of the ankle. That is all. I fell down, a day before... In a few days I will be better... *(TO DEREK)* She said nothing. Her eyes were looking at my dish of rice from breakfast... Laid out for my feast game... *(TO GRAHAM)* I was playing feasts...
GRAHAM:	I've never played feasts... What do you do?

KAMALA:	*(TO DEREK)* And I showed her how to play feasts... It is very easy... I take the rice my mother had cooked and left for me... And put it onto little heaps...
	This heap here... This is lentils... This is chicken... This is lamb... And every little heap is part of the great feast...
GRAHAM:	I'll put my cashew nuts in...
KAMALA:	This is Dosay... These are vegetable Bajha... And chutney... *(GIVING GRAHAM A TASTE OF ONE OF THE HEAPS OF RICE)*... Now try this... Is this chicken to your taste, lady?
GRAHAM:	*(TASTING)*... I think... More chili...
KAMALA:	*(TRYING IT)* Let me see... No... It's not hot enough... Try the bananas...
	(TO DEREK) You see... We were enjoying the feast so much... It had put the letter out of my mind... And I knew nothing about letters...
GRAHAM:	Do you want to hear what the letter says, then, Kamala?
KAMALA:	Let me see this letter... *(SHE TAKES IT... EXAMINES IT... FEELS IT WITH HER FINGERS...)* This is for me?...
GRAHAM:	It comes from a boy in Jarrow... In England... One of the holy places in England.
KAMALA:	*(TO DEREK)* After I had heard your letter, I couldn't wait to answer you and tell you about my life... Now I knew the Jesus woman was not a government woman and we had played the Feast game together, my eyes were opened to her... The Jesus woman is a pleasant woman... I say this to her ears, because she is writing this down in my letter to you. She speaks Tamil not too goodly. But quite goodly.
GRAHAM:	I thought I spoke it reasonably well, Kamala...
KAMALA:	I can understand it, lady... *(DICTATING TO DEREK)* *My dear English friend, Derek.* I have never heard of Jarrow, your home. I do not like the sound of the name. Miss Graham says it's a holy place... I live in *not such a holy place.* Korrukupet... I am Kamala... Korrukupet is near Madras... It is huts people have built on a flat piece of land where the Madras people throw all their rubbish. Every day, big lorries come full of the rubbish the Madras people who live in houses have thrown away... They dump it round our huts... I had a fever... Many years ago... And the strength went from my legs... My mother and my sister work in Madras, carrying bricks... They go out from the hut very early in the morning, while I am

full of sleep and they will not return till the dark comes... If you go down on the ground *(DEREK DOES THIS)* and dream the strength has gone from your legs... you will have a picture of me... If you push down very hard on the ground... Can you see what happens... You can make your body move with your hands... If you will do this, you will see this is not such a bad thing as people imagine... I can move about the house... eat the rice my mother has left... look at the books of pictures my sister brings me, that the Madras rich people throw away... So you will have a picture of my life in your mind...

When the truth came to me that you were truly writing to me... A person across the world—thousands and thousands of miles from Madras had heard *my* name... And had thoughts about me. This was a good feeling... It was a new, happy good feeling...

(TO DEREK) I thank you for this... I thank you from very deep in my heart.

GRAHAM: I'll make sure this gets posted.

....
SHIRLEY IS LOOKING AT A POSTER FOR WHEELCHAIRS...

DEREK: *(TO KAMALA)*
Dear Kamala,
I can't stand being *organised*... Can you? Shirley spends her flaming life *organising*... I'm writing this letter in Newcastle Station... Shirley dragged me to this shop, Saturday morning looking for something for you...
(DEREK MOVES TO THE WHEELCHAIR.)

A hundred and forty flaming pounds!... Shirley man... Look at it... *A hundred and forty pounds!*

SHIRLEY: I hate them pictures there, of these cripples smiling like it was fantastic not being able to walk and having to use flaming wheelchairs.

DEREK: Still... It's a great chair, isn't it?... Bloke says it can go on all kinds of surfaces...

SHIRLEY: I suppose if they looked *desperate* in the picture, nobody'd want to buy the chairs... Look how miserable I am, in this flaming wheelchair.

DEREK: I've got about four pounds... How much have you?

SHIRLEY: Come on... better go...

DEREK: Could nick it, couldn't we?... I mean... It's just like robbing the rich to feed the poor, isn't it?

SHIRLEY:	Yeah, alright... Nick it... Go on...
DEREK:	Working out how you could do it...
SHIRLEY:	Stuff it under your jumper...
DEREK:	Tell the bloke... Want to try it outside... *You* keep him chatting... *I* run off with it...
SHIRLEY:	Come on...
DEREK:	Bloke says we could pay it up.. didn't he? Every week...
SHIRLEY:	With *what*?
DEREK:	Telling you, man... *You*... Everything's flaming impossible for you!
SHIRLEY:	He told you, man... Your dad would have to come and sign the flaming papers...
DEREK:	Dead... Say me Dad's dead.
SHIRLEY:	Your Mam.
DEREK:	The wheelchair's supposed to be for her, isn't it? How can she come in till she gets it?
SHIRLEY:	We'll go to the station... get a cup of coffee... and write an answer to Kamala's letter...
DEREK:	*(HANDLING CHAIR... LAST FOND LOOK)* I'm gonna get that chair for her... Telling you...
SHIRLEY:	Great... I hope it keeps fine for you...
DEREK:	Telling you... You've got find out every flaming thing under the sun before you even flaming *breathe*...
SHIRLEY:	Better to know what you're up against, isn't it?
DEREK:	You reckon?
	....
DEREK:	*(TO KAMALA)* Listen... I'd better tell you who *Shirley* is... I said I wouldn't tell any lies to you... But I told you a lie right in my first letter... *I didn't write* that letter... Shirley did... I mean... I told her what to put into it... Trouble is I can't flaming write... I mean... I can write a bit... But like it takes me fifty times as long as any of the other kids to write something... And after that nobody can flaming read it... *I* can't read it...
SHIRLEY:	Try and write that yourself, Derek, man...
DEREK:	I can't write, man... *(TO KAMALA)* I've started to really try and write, now... Shirley's lent me this spelling machine... It's great... *(PRESSES MACHINE...*

SPELLS OUT SOME BASIC WORDS)... I'm going to work on that an hour every night... Definitely... Till I learn every word in that... I am... And we've worked out how we're going to help you...

SHIRLEY: Derek, man... That's stupid... How have we?

DEREK: The wheelchair, man...

SHIRLEY: Derek... I'm not writing that... I'm not... They cost hundreds of pounds... That's stupid, promising her something we can't do...

DEREK: I'm telling you, Shirley... We will... we will get her one.

SHIRLEY: Nuh!.. That's stupid... Raising her hopes like that... I'm not writing it... Nuh...

DEREK: That's what we're going to do, Shirley, man... I know... We're gonna get her a wheelchair...

SHIRLEY: Yeah... Well when we've *got* one... *then* we can tell her...

DEREK: Telling her about the day I wrote to her... Right?...
(TO KAMALA)
You see... It was great, wasn't it... I found out your name... And this woman to send the letters to... Miss Graham... In Madras, India... Bought this writing pad in the shopping centre... and nicked the pen... Cost me 30p for the paper... I'm sitting in front of the pad... I'd got down 'Dear Kamala'... I could write that alright... Mind, I wasn't sure if anybody could read it... I'd wasted seven rotten sheets of paper... I mean... I was full of all the kinds of things... And I just couldn't get them out... I couldn't write them down... I was *sick*... I was getting sicker...
I tried to write all kinds of things I wanted to tell you... and it just came out... Rubbish... 'Dear Kamala, I am twelve years old... I go to school in Jarrow'... Rubbish like that... 'I support Sunderland F.C.'... You couldn't even read what I'd written, anyway... *I* couldn't read it...
In the end, I gave up... Getting on my nerves trying to write a letter. Worse than flaming school... *(SCREWS UP PAPER. THROWS IT AWAY.)* Stuff it! Who wants to waste their time writing stupid flaming letters to Darkies in rotten India you've never heard of...

DEREK: *(TO KAMALA)*
...I put me jacket on and went out to have some fun... It was too windy for Charlie's Park so I ended up at the Moving Staircases... There's a tunnel there. It's great. Runs right under the river Tyne... That's how you get down to it... On this Moving Staircase... I start walking along the tunnel,

when I saw Shirley, coming back from Howdon. She's got an Auntie there...

You see... I'd kind of given up the whole idea of writing to you... Too much bother... Then I saw Shirley... I mean... I liked her... I fancied her... All the boys in our class fancy her... She's got nice hair and her face and that... And she's always wearing dead smart gear... I mean... I've been waiting to ask her to go out with me for years... But everybody was after her... And I know I'm not much cop... am I?... This time... I don't know what came over me... I made up my mind *then*, seeing her... I was going to ask her to go out with me, *this* time...

DEREK:	*(TO SHIRLEY)* Where are you going?
SHIRLEY:	What's it to you?
DEREK:	*(TO KAMALA)* Just walked past me... *(TO SHIRLEY)* Shirley...
SHIRLEY:	What do you want?
DEREK:	I want to speak to you.
SHIRLEY:	What for?
DEREK:	What for?
DEREK:	*(TO KAMALA)* Trying to think of something to say. I never knew what to say to *her*... You never know what to say to girls, do you? *(TO SHIRLEY)* I want to speak to you, man...
SHIRLEY:	What for?
DEREK:	What do you keep saying 'what for' for?
SHIRLEY:	Because you flaming won't tell me what for?
DEREK:	*(TO KAMALA)* So I'm kind of walking along with her... Working out what to say to her...
SHIRLEY:	You following me, Derek Bates?
DEREK:	Nuh... I'm going along the tunnel...
SHIRLEY:	Do you need to go along the bit I'm going along.
DEREK:	*(TO KAMALA)* Then... Because it was something to say to her... I told her about you... Trying to write to you... She got interested...
SHIRLEY:	How can *you* write letters to India? You *can't* flaming *write*...
DEREK:	I'm telling you. I can't write so good... Nuh... That's what I told you...
SHIRLEY:	You can't write your *name*, Derek Bates...
DEREK:	I can write me name...

SHIRLEY:	Just...
DEREK:	*(TO KAMALA)* Then she kind of took everything over... That's what she's like... She can do things... The teacher's always getting her to organise things in the class...
SHIRLEY:	I know what we'll do... You tell me what you want to write to her and I'll write it down... Like being a secretary... You'll have to come over to my house... Because I'm not going to yours... Me Mam wouldn't like me going to your house... You come tomorrow, after school... But you'll need to put on clean trousers...and have you a jumper that hasn't got holes in it, so you don't look a right scruff... Just for me Mam...
DEREK:	*(TO KAMALA)* When we got outside, we were still walking... together... Walking home, she said to me:
SHIRLEY:	When you stopped me down in the tunnel, before... I thought you were going to ask me to go out with you...
DEREK:	Did you?
SHIRLEY:	If you want... I might...
DEREK:	Would you?
SHIRLEY:	Do you want to?
DEREK:	Yeah?
SHIRLEY:	You'd have to get rid of that earring... I don't like lads with earrings... And you could do with washing your hair...
DEREK:	*(TO KAMALA)* She stopped... Looking at me... Waiting...
SHIRLEY:	Well?
DEREK:	Well what, man?
SHIRLEY:	Make up your mind... Do you want to go out with me?...
DEREK:	Alright...
SHIRLEY:	Do you?
DEREK:	I said 'yeah', man... Didn't I?
SHIRLEY:	Alright. I'll think about it... I'll tell you tomorrow when we write that letter
	....
KAMALA:	*(WITH A HEAVY STICK. WAVING IT AT GRAHAM)* You go away from here! You don't come in here. Never again, you come in here.
GRAHAM:	I've got another letter for you, Kamala.
KAMALA:	I don't care about your damn letters. I'll tell you about your letters. Your letters bring me nothing but damn trouble. Tha

boy and your damn Jesus letters. Take away your white ghost face from my house, this minute, when I tell you.

GRAHAM: I'm going. If that's what you want. There's the letter...
(THROWING IT TO HER)

KAMALA: What good is that damn letter to me, you white ghost face lying Jesus vulture. You know I can't damn read, Jesus woman.

GRAHAM: What do you want me to do, Kamala? Will I go or stay and read the letter... Make up your mind.

KAMALA: It's alright. I hate you. I hate the sight of you in my eyes... I'm finished with you. I'm not a Jesus woman like you. I *hate* my enemies. I *hate* you. Go away from my house.

GRAHAM: Kamala... Listen... I'm sorry... I was held up in Madras... I was going to meet up with her here and we were going to see you together...

KAMALA: You're supposed to be my friend, Jesus woman, and you send witch women to me.

GRAHAM: She's a health worker, Kamala... She's not a doctor or a nurse or anything medical... Just another community worker like me... That's all...

KAMALA: She's a witch woman. I know that...

GRAHAM: It wasn't even an official visit. I happened to talk about you...

KAMALA: I hate you....I'm finished with you... Go away... Get out of the sight of my eyes... I can't stand to look at your lying white Jesus face.

GRAHAM: Listen. Do you not think it might be a good idea if you told me what I'm supposed to have done.

KAMALA: I hate you. I'm finished with you... I'm not a Jesus woman like you. I hate my enemies... Go away... Get out of the sight of my eyes... I can't stand to look at your white lying face... Go away... You send me that witch woman...

GRAHAM: That was a Health worker... She was trying to help you, you stupid, suspicious fool...

KAMALA: Yes. Help me out of this world.
I know very well how witch women help people!
Thank you. I will go out of this world in God's time...
(TO DEREK)
I nearly didn't read your letter, telling me you had found a way to help me. I had so much bad anger in me... When the Jesus woman came, it was bursting out from me so much, I could have pulled the letter from her hand and torn it to

pieces with my teeth... The Jesus woman says I have very much anger in me... But now it is out... *(TO GRAHAM)* I've thrown it all over you, Jesus woman...

GRAHAM: I didn't like the way you were waving that stick, Kamala...

KAMALA: It could've broken your head, Jesus woman...

GRAHAM: What are you frightened of, Kamala? Tell me... What terrible things do you think thta woman was going to do to you?

KAMALA: I am frightened... I am very frightened... You know what I am frightened about...

(TO DEREK) The day before I write this letter... Now this is a good luck... I don't know what would have happened if I wouldn't have had that good luck...

GRAHAM: Nothing would've happened... People are trying to help you, Kamala...

KAMALA: People tried to help my father...

GRAHAM: Your father had tuberculosis... That's a fatal disease... If he could have got help quicker...

KAMALA: *(TO DEREK)* She doesn't know that, and she can read... and she can write... In English and Tamil... She reads books... And she is an ignorant woman. *(TO GRAHAM)* In these things you are very ignorant, Jesus woman... The hospital killed my father...

GRAHAM: If that's what you have to believe... Go on... The earth is flat.. The moon is made of coca cola...

KAMALA: That you know about... You are very clever about these things... I am not troubled... The earth is flat as far as I can see... *You* don't know about hospitals... *You* don't know what happened to my father... *I* know what happened to my father... That's why I hid from that woman...

(TO DEREK) I tell you about the luck I have... No person passed me to take me to the latrines... Only Nukand was sitting there... Like he sits sometimes... Waiting for me to look at him... He has no right to sit where our huts are... He is a filthy untouchable... He is always staring at me... and smiling at me... I am so desperate to go to the latrines and so full of anger at the sight of him... There is a dead rat near my hand... I throw it at him... with all my strength... It strikes him on the face... And he runs away... In the end, full of desperation... I go myself to the latrines... When I am crawling back... This is lucky... I crawl back and the lady does not see me.

(THE WOMAN FROM THE HEALTH AUTHORITIES IS AT THE DOORWAY)

WOMAN: Can I come in?

KAMALA: *(TO DEREK)* She can go in if she pleases... I am not here to be found by her long prodding nose and poking eyes...

WOMAN: May I come in?

KAMALA: *(TO DEREK)* And she has no politeness... She is like a great deal of government people... They have a strange sense of politeness... She walks in without being asked to come in... I am hiding behind another hut... *I* know these things... This is not a good woman... This is a witch woman...

GRAHAM: Kamala... You are being stupid, woman... Listen... I know... I can see now... You're a bright, intelligent child...

KAMALA: *(TO DEREK)* She goes into my hut... and is poking her long government nose into our private things...

(WOMAN COMES OUT OF HUT)

At last she comes out... From poking about our hut... She looks about her... Then looks at the papers in her hands... All these government people have papers... they see nothing else... In the hospital my father went to... My mother says... There, too, they were looking at papers... He had a bed in the hospital... An iron bed... At the bottom of the bed, she told me, there was papers at the bottom of the bed... The first thing the doctors looked at when they came to his bed... was the papers... I know all about papers...

(TO DEREK) She looks all round her... I am hiding outside... I will be honest with you, boy, I am very afraid... I am shaking with being afraid... *(WOMAN LOOKS ROUND... THEN GIVES UP)*... Then she goes away... I wait behind Jagran's hut... an hour, maybe... Till I am sure she is not returning... Then I go back to my hut again... And do you know who sent that damn witch to my house... That Jesus woman who is supposed to be my friend...

GRAHAM: To help you, woman!

KAMALA: *(TO DEREK)* To take me to hospital in the city and kill me... like my father... That's how these people help you...

GRAHAM: ... Kamala... How can I come here, woman, and not try to help you...

KAMALA: I have a person to help me... He lives in this holy place... and he has promised to help me...
You help me by keeping witches away from my house, lady...

You must promise this to me... Listen to me... I have no
sleep... Do you know this... All night I have no sleep... For
fear of you sending more witches to my house... You have
shadowed my life, friend... I know in my heart you are my
friend... Please... Miss Graham... Don't shadow my life like
this...

GRAHAM: I can't handle *you*... Do you know that... I don't know what t
do with you... I want to *help* you, for God's sake...

*DEREK WHEELS OUT HIS BIKE. LAYS OUT HIS TOOLS,
SLOWLY... RELUCTANTLY. SHIRLEY WATCHES HIM. HE
APPROACHES THE BIKE... LIFTS A SPANNER... THEN
DRAWS BACK...*

SHIRLEY: Go on... Start the operation.

DEREK: It's my bike. Flaming wouldn't let me use *yours*.

SHIRLEY: Mine is brand new. Yours is a flaming wreck, isn't it?

DEREK: Goes.

SHIRLEY: *Just.*

DEREK: *(CONSIDERING THE PATHETIC MACHINE)* Yeah... *(HALF-
HEARTEDLY ATTACKS A WHEEL NUT... THEN GIVES UP)*
Shirley... I *need* my bike, man, don't I? I like going to
Shields... and runs like that...

SHIRLEY: I know. Forget it... Come on... We'll write to Kamala...

DEREK: I mean... If I hadn't my bike, I'd be stuck in Jarrow.

SHIRLEY: Anyway... How could you make a wheelchair out of a bike..

DEREK: Easy, man... Just need the big wheels... and a frame... and
seat and that... Nuh... I havn't got all the parts, have I?... I
mean... and there's the money to send it to India... Why
couldn't she live in rotten *Gateshead*!

... *You* could sell *your* bike, Shirley

SHIRLEY: And get murdered by me Mam... I need my bike. I like it...

DEREK: If I'd had the parts... I could've made it... Telling you...
(SHIRLEY TURNS AWAY) Don't believe me, do you?

SHIRLEY: Nuh...

DEREK: Don't believe in nowt, do you?

Come on... We'll start the letter...
(TO KAMALA) Dear Kamala,
I want to tell you how I was so sick, that day the man from
India came...

SHIRLEY: Yeah... Why were you so sick, Derek?

DEREK:	Going to tell you, aren't I?
	(TO KAMALA) I couldn't tell you or Shirley this before... I don't know why... See... It was me Mam and Dad... like... When I was dead young... I think Dad went off... for a year or something... Then he came back again... I can't remember about it... Anyway... That night... Before the man from India came... It's my Mam's birthday... Dad was sitting in front of the telly, playing Space Invaders... It's a telly game... about saving the Universe... I'm dead good at it... Always beating Dad... Mam's getting ready to go to the club...
	(MAM COMES IN WITH HAIR DRYER)
MAM:	Derek, pet, can you get at the back of me hair, love...
DEREK:	*(TO KAMALA)* So... I'm drying Mam's hair... She looks dead nice... She says to Dad...
MAM:	You want to come with me tonight, Roy?
DAD:	Angela, man... What's the point, eh?
MAM:	Probably you're right... Yes...
DEREK:	*(TO KAMALA)* Dad... you see... has a girlfriend... across the road... *I* don't understand it... She's not half as nice looking as me Mam... I don't know how he fancies her better than Mam... Mam went in to put her dress on... I said to Dad, feeling dead sorryfor Mam... going to the club on her own on her birthday...
DEREK:	Dad... It's her birthday...
DAD:	I *know*, man...
DEREK:	Not fancy taking her to the club...
	(TO KAMALA) And we have this understanding session... Always having them understanding sessions... Where Mam or Dad kind of try to get me to understand what's going on in their minds...
DAD:	See... Now... Sheila... This is her night when she goes out and does old biddies' hair... Isn't it?...
DEREK:	yeah...
DAD:	Telling you, man... So... Like if I took your Mam to the Club... and Sheila heard about it... You know... She's working... and I'm raving it up with yer Mam at the Club... I mean... Sheila's out doing her good deeds for the day... She is, isn't she?... It's not right, is it?
DEREK:	*(TO KAMALA)* yeah...
DAD:	Come on give us another game...

DEREK:	It's boring, Dad... I always beat you...
DAD:	I know... How do you do that?
DEREK:	*(TO KAMALA)* Mam came in... Dressed... She did... She looked dead nice... I saw me Dad looking at her, too... In her pink blouse and high heel shoes and make-up... She kind of stood in front of Dad...
MAM:	Sure you don't want to go, then?...
DEREK:	*(TO KAMALA)* Dad kept looking at Mam... Not saying anything for a bit...
DAD:	Angela, you know man... Don't you?...
MAM:	You're right, yeah... *(GOING)* There's 20p for chips...
DAD:	*(TO MAM)* Spare another fifty for a supper for me, Angela...
DEREK:	*(TO KAMALA)* Took out a pound note from her bag... It's her that's working and got the money, you see... since Dad was finished at the steel works...
MAM:	*(GOING)* I'll bring you back a bottle of Ginger Ale... that's what you like, isn't it?...
DEREK:	Great, Mam.
	(TO KAMALA) Dad was hunched over the telly, saving the Universe...
	(TO DAD) Dad... Don't play that all night, man... I want to see the Professionals...
	(TO KAMALA) In the end... I went to bed... I couldn't sleep... Dad started playing Space Invaders again... Flaming Invaders spaceships and rockets kept flying into my dreams and waking me up... I heard me Dad come upstairs into my room... It's 12.04 in the morning...
DAD:	You still up, Derek?...
DEREK:	Yeah... *(TO KAMALA)* I'm watching the clock ticking away the seconds... Dad sees it too...
DAD:	I don't like these digital clocks... You know... Ticking away at the seconds of your life... One second less... Another second less... Not good... Listen... If you're not sleeping... Fancy making me a toasted sandwich... I never get them right...
DEREK:	*(TO KAMALA)* So I go in and get the sandwich maker out... and start making him a toasted cheese and onion sandwich... Dad bought it for Mam... when he was finished at the steel works and got all that redundancy money...
DAD:	Fancy a game... If you can't sleep... Have a couple games... Tire you out...

DEREK: *(TO KAMALA)* Like, all the exercise of twiddling the knobs and watching the screen...

So that was how Mam found us... You see... About one o'clock in the morning... Dad had been at the beer... Cans all over the carpet... All the smoke of his tabs... Room was looking like the Space Invaders had got our house... And they both were a bit drunk... Could see it in her look... You know?...

(TO KAMALA) All the noise of Space Invaders going... and the mess of Dad's beer... and the fish and chips paper... She didn't shout or anything... She just walked over the Space Invaders control box... Threw it off the table... And kind of trampled on it. *(SHE DOES THIS)* Not saying anything... Dad got up... Not saying anything either...
... He smashed her across the face... I tried to stop him... and come between them... but he pushed me away...

DEREK: Dad!... Man, leave her alone...

(TO KAMALA) Then he said... Still nobody shouting or anything...

DAD: Right, then... I'm finished... That's it...

DEREK: *(TO KAMALA)* And he just walked out the house... In the middle of the night... In his shirt, didn't even take his jacket... he just walked out... I picked up the photograph me Mam had knocked off the television set... came out of its frame... I had to push it back again... I was nearly crying... I stopped meself in case Mam came back... It was the worst feeling I'd ever had in me life... I was losing Dad... I knew it... He was never going to come back... I tried to push it out of my mind... Kept saying to meself he would be back in the morning... Just a row we've had, that's all... My mind kept wandering round in circles... I've lost me Dad...

GRAHAM: *(CALLING)* Kamala... It's Miss Graham... Can I come in?

KAMALA: *(TO DEREK)* Miss Graham came when I was busy making myself beautiful for your photograph...

(TO GRAHAM) Please to wait outside, for a moment, lady...

DEREK: Look... She's sent me a photograph...

SHIRLEY: Let's see...

DEREK: It's nice...

SHIRLEY: Let us *see*, man...

KAMALA: *(TO DEREK)* My sister had great luck... She went out to search through the rubbish... And she found some make-up from some rich woman in Madras... There was very much lipstick left... and this was beautiful... Miss Graham has a camera that makes pictures coloured... and you will be abl to see...

GRAHAM: What are you doing in there, Kamala?...

KAMALA: I wil not keep you long, lady... You are so busy... I will not e up your time... I am nearly finished...

(TO DEREK) My mother left out her holiday sari... it was a present from my father, when he once went to work for tw whole years in Bombay... and brought back this Bombay sari... Do you like it?

SHIRLEY: She looks dead nice... doesn't she?... Do you fancy her?...

KAMALA: You may enter my house, now, Miss Jesus woman...

GRAHAM: *That's* what you've been doing?

KAMALA: Is this good?... I am in a very happy mood...

GRAHAM: That's good...

KAMALA: You see... You believe nothing... Do you know what happened?... This morning... when I woke up... Listen to this... My legs were twingling... That is what happened this morning... I had feeling in the skin... Like I was lying on a be of thorns...

(TO DEREK) When I felt this... My heart was singing with joy... At first I thought this was a dream... I was dreaming th feeling... But when it came to me I was awake...

GRAHAM: Kamala... You must see a damn doctor, woman,... I'm tellin you...

KAMALA: You dare bring doctors to my house, Jesus woman...

GRAHAM: You don't want to walk again... Alright, forget it...

KAMALA: I will walk again... I know that... Without your damn doctors.

GRAHAM: I'll take your photograph...

KAMALA: Listen... I want to talk to you, lady... I want you to help me. lady... I have decided... I wish to go to school...

GRAHAM: I spoke to you about this before... You need to go to school

KAMALA: I am telling you... I wish to go to school...

(TO DEREK) This was an even stranger thing than the feelin coming to my legs... A day was a day... Do you understand me? Every day was like being born and dying at the end o it... My life stretched only from the morning of my rising to

the night when I passed into sleep... Do you understand this?

GRAHAM: Yes, I think he will...

KAMALA: *(TO DEREK)* This is surely a God thing that was happened... Sitting in our hut... Eating the morning rice... Mother had made it with some raisins she had bought and fat... It was very good... It added to my happy feelings... Sitting enjoying my morning rice, I found myself... looking beyond the end of the day... the end of the week,.. or the year... Now I knew the strength would come back to my legs again and I would walk...

GRAHAM: Kamala... I'm worried about the way you're fixing your hopes on this child in England... I'm very worried...

KAMALA: *(TO DEREK)* Now... I knew this... The thought came to me... No, I decided... I would not go to Madras and carry bricks and wood... like my mother and sister... to build houses for rich people... I will not do that, I said to myself... What I will do... Because I know now how good it is and important it is to be able to put your thoughts on paper... and read the thoughts of other people... I will first go to school and I will study and when I have learned this reading and writing... Then I will teach others like me, so that they, too, will be able to read and write... Do you think this is good a idea?...

GRAHAM: If you're sensible... It's an excellent idea...

KAMALA: Will you help me to go to school, lady?

GRAHAM: If you'd let that woman in, from the Health services... I'm talking about getting you to school... If I can find you a place... That's what I am talking about... I think there is somewhere I can find a place for you... But it's miles away, woman... At least a mile... Bit more... Look at you... How are you going to cope with two miles there and back every day...

KAMALA: When I can walk again... It will be easy...

GRAHAM: *Till* you can walk... I'm talking about...

KAMALA: Believe me, lady... I will *walk*... I know.
You help me to find a place in school... Believe me... I would be very grateful... Please, lady... Help me to go to school... I know... Believe me... You please make arrangements for me to go to school... I will *get* there...

GRAHAM: I'd better read you the letter.

KAMALA: Please. Take my photograph first.

GRAHAM: I'll talk to the people in the school... Ready?

111

KAMALA:	I would like to stand, please... If you lift me so I can hold on to the ring from the ceiling... *(SHE LIFTS HER GENTLY... SHE STRETCHES HER HAND TO HOLD ON TO A RING FROM THE ROOF... SUPPORTED BY THIS AND PARTLY BY THE WALL... SHE STANDS, SMILING... FLASH OF GRAHAM'S CAMERA)*
	(DEREK IS WHEELING A BATTERED WHEELCHAIR TOWARDS SHIRLEY)
DEREK:	I got a wheelchair...
SHIRLEY:	Wow!
DEREK:	From the W.V.S... I said it was for me sister... broke her leg...
SHIRLEY:	I hope she likes it...
DEREK:	I haven't *got* a sister, you know that... Shirley... I've got a *chair*, man... Look... Why do you always keep knocking everything I do... Look! *(TRYING IT)* Goes great... doesn't it?
SHIRLEY:	What are you going to do with it?
DEREK:	I've *got* it... I found about the W.V.S. lending chairs...
SHIRLEY:	What good's *that* to Kamala?
DEREK:	Shirley... We'll work something out... Telling you... Main thing is, we've got a chair for Kamala...
SHIRLEY:	I keep telling you... This is Jarrow, man... Not *Fairyland*... What are you going to *do*?... Nick that chair and send it to India?
DEREK:	I've got the *chair*...
SHIRLEY:	You're gonna send it to India...
DEREK:	I told you... I'll work something out, man...
SHIRLEY:	Like *what*?
DEREK:	*(TO KAMALA)* I don't know what it is... I get everything worked out... and flaming Shirely comes along and smashes everything to pieces... I wish I was like you... The way you always know what you want to do and do it... I mean... I don' think you're right about doctors... But I don't like them either... I found this thing for you... I can't tell you what it is... Shirley won't let me... Anyway... Shirley and me had this fight over it... So I took it back to my house... *(STRUGGLING TO FOLD IT... TO TAKE IT INTO THE HOUSE... GIVING UP)* *(DRAGGING IT ALONG)* Just taking it to hide in me room... mean... I don't know how I was going to hide it... When me Mam shouts for me... Trouble is, you see, she's a warden looking after old people... and you can never be sure *when* she comes home...

MAM: Derek!

DEREK: *(TO KAMALA)* She was making a cake... Her new mixer must've come... I could see she was in a mood... So I tried to get her off whatever track she was on...
(TO MAM) You've a new mixer, Mam...

MAM: I want to *talk* to you, Derek... What's that?

DEREK: Just for Kamala, Mam... I picked it up...

MAM: Have you been messing about the rubbish tip, Derek?

DEREK: I got in a *shop*, Mam... Just a few pounds...

MAM: Derek... You *promised* me... you wouldn't go inside that woman's house... Get that out of here, Derek... I'm preparing food... You don't know what the person had who used that chair...

DEREK: Mam, it's dead clean... Look at it...

MAM: I'm talking about you going into that woman's house...

DEREK: I didn't, Mam... I didn't go to Sheila's house

MAM: I can't stand that... You calling her 'Sheila' to my face, Derek...

DEREK: No, Mam... *(TO KAMALA)* I mean... like... That's her *name*... What else did she want me to call her...

MAM: Will you throw that horrible thing out the house, Derek... It upsets me... The smell of it...

DEREK: Yeah, Mam... Sending it to Kamala...

MAM: You *promised* me... Didn't you?

DEREK: Mam, I didn't go to her house...

MAM: Don't, Derek. Don't tell lies to me. You don't need to tell lies to me, love. That's not *you* and me, is it, Derek? I *know*... I've been told... Will you get that miserable wheelchair out of here...

DEREK: *(GOING)* Yeah... I'll put it...

MAM: Where are you going? I'm speaking to you, man... You know how much it upsets me, the idea of you in her house... And you still go there...

DEREK: I don't, Mam...

MAM: Get that out, Derek, please...
(HE IS ABOUT TO GO) Come here, Derek...

DEREK:	*(TO KAMALA)* Had me flaming dizzy... I went to her and she took my hands... And looked into my eyes... *(TO MAM)* I like seeing Dad, Mam... That's all... That's why I go... You know that...
MAM:	Don't tell me lies, son. Promise me... Whatever you do. You'll never tell me lies again...
DEREK:	*(TO KAMALA)* And she was going on to have an under-standing session again...
MAM:	I know it's difficult for you, pet. You like seeing your Dad... That's natural... I'll get over it, probably... in time... But just now... The idea of you in that woman's house... Do you have *food* there? Does she give you meals?
DEREK:	*(TO KAMALA)* Went on for *hours*... What I did in Sheila's... Did she give me money... Didn't want to stop me seeing Dad... I could see him in a cafe... Going round and round in flaming circles... Driving me round the bend... Didn't know where I flaming was... In the end... I promised her...
DEREK:	Nuh... I won't go there again, Mam... I promise you... Kept it up for nearly *two* hours... Till I passed Sheila's house... That night after tea... And just couldn't kind of stop myself going in to see Dad... Told you... I didn't know where I flaming was...
DAD:	What's that?
DEREK:	It's a wheelchair, Dad...
DAD:	What you bringing that in here for?
DEREK:	*(TO KAMALA)* One of these days you couldn't talk to Dad... Anything you'd say to him... Couldn't say 'good morning' to him... That would upset him... All I said was...

Can I keep it here, Dad... You know?Till I find out how to send it to India?...

(TO KAMALA) That started him off... I asked *him*, you see... Not Sheila... Sheila was standing there... She went out... I'm sure she went out to make the tea... Dad worked it out I'd upset her... |
DAD:	Derek. *You* know whose house this is. It's *Sheila's* house. You ask *her*, if you want to leave anything here...
DEREK:	I'll ask her, Dad. Alright... I'll go and ask her...
DAD:	Listen, son... I'll tell you something... The way you to talk to her... It upset me...
DEREK:	I didn't talk to her, Dad, man... Didn't say a word to her...

DAD:	That's what I am saying... The way you don't say a word to her... You ignore her...
DEREK:	*(TO KAMALA)* Just went from bad to worse...
DAD:	And the way Sheila's always thinking of you... Just saying, a minute ago... You need a haircut... If you turned up she'd give you a haircut...
DEREK:	I don't need a haircut... *(TO KAMALA)* Always messing about with people's hair, Sheila... Had this thing about people's hair...
DAD:	She's going to give you a haircut, son.
DEREK:	Dad... I don't need a haircut... I need all the hair I have...
DAD:	You need a trim, man. Look at you.
DEREK:	I don't want her messing about my hair, man... She's always messing about with people's hair...
DAD:	There you are... You're at it again... Getting at Sheila...
DEREK:	Dad, I just don't want her to cut my hair...
DAD:	Derek. Calm down, son... Just calm down...
DEREK:	I don't *need* a haircut...
DAD:	Just calm down, son... I want to talk to you...
DEREK:	*(TO KAMALA)* Flipping hell! Another flaming understanding session...
DAD:	Fair enough... Nobody can blame you... It hasn't worked out the way you wanted it... That's what happened... Now... Listen to me... You can't force people to like other people... Sheila likes you... That's her... You can't take to Sheila just now... Fair enough... I'm not asking you to do that... All I'm asking is that you treat Sheila with a bit of courtesy... That's all... That's all I'm asking...
DEREK:	I do Dad, man...
DAD:	It gets me, Derek. You know that. It eats into me at times, the way you treat Sheila... And how much she thinks of you... Do you know that... See what she got for you there... Went all round Newcastle, looking for that for you.
DEREK:	*(TO KAMALA)* It was great. Smashing sweater... Seen other kids with them... Dying for one for months... Made me feel real rotten... The way I sometimes hated Sheila... And all the things she bought me and did for me... Dad was holding it out for me...
DAD:	Go on, man... Try it on...

DEREK:	I put it on... It was great... Just fitted me right and everything...
DAD:	What do you think, then?
DEREK:	It's great, Dad... Smashing...
DAD:	You not going into the kitchen to thank Sheila for it, then...
DEREK:	Yeah... I'll go, Dad...
	Gave me this funny feeling... Going in to thank Sheila... In my stomach... I mean... I know... It was dead good of her... I knew that... Giving me that sweater and everything... I don't know *why* I couldn't flaming stand thanking her for it...

....

(GRAHAM IS CARRYING KAMALA ON HER SHOULDER... EXHAUSTED, SHE GENTLY PUTS HER DOWN ON THE FLOOR OF THE HUT...)

KAMALA:	*(TO DEREK)* Do you know this is my last letter to you... Or it might be my last letter... I will never write to you again... I hope I will write to you again... I am frightened this will be the truth... Miss Graham comes to me, this morning, very stubborn... She tells me...
GRAHAM:	I'm taking you to the school.
KAMALA:	That is good. Why are you looking with such a stern face at me... This is a very happy day for me... Isn't it a happy day for me... You are taking me to school... My dreams are turning to truth.
	(TO DEREK) Still this Miss Graham does not smile. She keeps her face still and eyes cold...
GRAHAM:	No... Your dreams are staying dreams, Kamala... I am going to take you to see this school... The two of us are going to make this mile journey to the school and the mile back to Korrukupet...
KAMALA:	*(TO DEREK)* She lifted me on her back and we began the journey... She had to stop many times to rest. She said it was only a mile to the school from Korrukupet... I am not sure... It seemed a very long mile... It might have been because there was anger between us, all the journey... And hardly any talk... Only once, when we stopped for a drink...
GRAHAM:	Do you want a drink?
KAMALA:	Please do not trouble yourself over me, lady.
GRAHAM:	Don't be so damned polite, Kamala. Do you *want* some?... I need a drink... That's for sure...

KAMALA: *(TO DEREK)* It was warm... But it was a drink... Drinking together seemed to take away some of the anger between us...

GRAHAM: *(CARRYING HER)* Are you comfortable, up there?

KAMALA: I am very comfortable, thank you... I am sorry I am such a heavy burden to you, lady...

GRAHAM: That's what you are... It's my choice to carry you here...

KAMALA: *(TO DEREK)* At last we came to the schoolhouse...

GRAHAM: There you are! Your dream school...

KAMALA: I see it...

GRAHAM: It's a *long* way, a mile... Did you realise how long a mile is, Kamala?

KAMALA: It seems a long way indeed, Miss Graham. Can we go inside and speak to the teachers...

GRAHAM: There's some water left... *(OFFERING IT TO HER)*

KAMALA: They are singing... Can you hear the singing?

GRAHAM: Kamala... Listen to me... I want to talk to you, a minute... What it is, you see, is... I *do*... I really believe that... You have some kind of knack of pulling me into your dreams...

KAMALA: That's good, isn't it... To bring others into your dreams... Is that no good?

GRAHAM: It could be me... I don't know... What I am talking about is *I* should be helping you to live in the world as it really is... Shouldn't I?... Instead of letting you carry me off to fairyland with you...

KAMALA: That is why you are angry with me... I take you into my dreams...

GRAHAM: I wasn't angry with you... How could I be angry with you... I am sorry... if you felt I was angry with you... I am really sorry... I wasn't at all...

KAMALA: That's good... That makes me feel good, now... You looked angry with me... It seemed that you were angry with me...

GRAHAM: You know me... That's me... The only one I ever seem to get really angry with is myself... I was angry, Yes... You're right... It bothers me... The way I've gone along with you... helping you with these letters to England... I don't think they're good for you, Kamala...

KAMALA: *(TO DEREK)* I knew this... I was sure of this.

(TO GRAHAM) Miss Graham... They are good for me... They are very good for me...

GRAHAM:	Kamala... You see what it's like... That mile from your hut... I wanted you to understand how long a real mile is, Kamala...
KAMALA:	It's a long way...
GRAHAM:	Who's going to carry you that mile to school every day and the mile back home, Kamala?
KAMALA:	I don't know, Miss Graham...
GRAHAM:	Kamala... We've got to... The pair of us... We've got to get out of this dream, haven't we? Your friend in Jarrow's not going to get you wings to fly the mile to school and the mile back to Korrukupet, is he?
KAMALA:	Listen... I am very happy now, Miss Graham... We are friends again... That's all that is filling my mind, just now... And going into the school... I would like to see the school and talk to the teachers, Miss Graham...
GRAHAM:	What for, Kamala?That's a real mile... It's not a dream mile... You're not going to make that mile, Kamala... You know it... Come on, Kamala... Are you? That's what a friend is for... We don't tell each other fairy tales...
KAMALA:	Is that lie then, Miss Graham?... It is not a holy place... Where the boy lives...
GRAHAM:	You see... I don't know what I should do, Kamala... I think we should stop writing to England... I don't think it's good for you, Kamala...
KAMALA:	Is it not a holy place, then?
GRAHAM:	I told you... It is a holy place... One holy place... Look at all the holy places in India... and round the world... Vishnu's a holy god... He's not putting the strength back in your legs...
KAMALA:	I know this... It is very much trouble to you... Helping me to write to England, Miss Graham... I am sorry for all this trouble I give you...
GRAHAM:	I don't want you to be let down, Kamala... You seem to be putting so much hope in these letters...
KAMALA:	I would be very sad if I stopped writing to the boy, Miss Graham...
GRAHAM:	Yes... I can understand that... Yes... I'm not sure... It could be... In the long run, Kamala... It would be better for you... If we stopped writing...
KAMALA:	(TO DEREK) I was looking at the school... Not answering her...
GRAHAM:	Will we go into the school, now?

KAMALA: *(TO DEREK)* From where we sat, I could see through the windows into the school... Children were working... studying books... some writing... In part of the building, there was singing... And there were flowers and trees round the school... and the school was bright with fresh paint... It was like a happy dream... The whole sight of it... and the singing of the children... The smell of paint came to me... Miss Graham bent down to help to carry me into the school... And the feeling came to me that I should not go into that happy dream school today... The first time I would go through the door... It came to me... would be when I started the school as a real student...

GRAHAM: After coming all this way you don't want to go on, Kamala... Kamala... What's the matter with you, woman...

KAMALA: I want to go home, Miss Graham... and write to the boy...
(TO DEREK)
And then Miss Graham said something which made me very angry... No... Very, very frightened... I don't know why it filled me with such fright...

GRAHAM: Listen, Kamala... I don't want to build your hopes too high... I've been trying for months to get you some kind of wheel-chair—and getting nowhere...

KAMALA: You were trying to get me into a wheelchair, lady?

GRAHAM: If we could get you a place in the school, Kamala...

KAMALA: Without speaking to me about this thing. You were planning to put me like a cripple without hope in his heart into a wheelchair...

GRAHAM: I am saying if we could get you into school, Kamala... There would be a stronger case...

KAMALA: Do not talk to me, Lady! Go away from me. I can't stand the sound of your ignorant voice grating into my ears... Go away from the sight of my eyes!

GRAHAM: Kamala... Where are you now, girl? I can't keep up with you...

KAMALA: You want to put me into a wheelchair... To take away all the hope from my heart...

GRAHAM: *(DEFEATED)* Kamala, Kamala, girl...

KAMALA: I say to her: I know this... I will walk on my two legs to this school... And she spits in my eye. I will put you into a wheelchair... I will turn you into a machine that can only move along the ground on wheels...

GRAHAM: *(GIVING UP... MOVED TOO BY KAMALA'S RESPONSE)*
I won't get you a wheelchair, Kamala. I am sorry... There was
hardly any chance of getting you one, anyway... I apologise
for even thinking about such a thing... I am sorry...

KAMALA: *(TO GRAHAM)* Listen... I will promise you... I will not trouble
you again to help me write to the boy... If nothing comes
from this letter to help me... we will write no more... And I
know... It is not likely anything will come to help me... I will
not be disappointed... My hopes are not too high, Miss
Graham.

(TO DEREK)
No... That is not the truth... I hope something will come from
your holy place to help me... I am not sure what could
come... I do not share your Jesus faith, anyway... But I will
write you what might be my very last letter anyway...

GRAHAM: Kamala... I'm not helping you... I'm sure of that... I'm not
helping you at all...

KAMALA: This woman... She gets so downcast and upset over her
friends... She worries so much... She should not worry so
much. I told her... *(TO GRAHAM)* Miss Graham, you should
not worry so much about your friends...

GRAHAM: You're right. You're absolutely right... I've got to make an
effort and do something about this...

(SHE TAKES HER ON HER SHOULDER... THEY MOVE OFF...)

KAMALA: *(TO DEREK)* We had a happy journey home. All the angry
feelings was burned out... To be truthful—or as Miss Graham
would say to come out of your dreams into the real world...
The mile home still was very long, although, this time, there
was nothing but good, happy friendship between us...

DEREK: *(TO SHIRLEY)* She doesn't *want a wheelchair*!
Shirley... She doesn't want a flaming wheelchair...

(TO KAMALA) Don't think this is a lump of rubbish I've sent
you in the envelope and throw it away... I'll tell you what it is
in a minute... And I am sorry the writing's not so good... I'm
writing this on my own... It's taken me flaming hours... I
mean... We started to write an answer to your letter,
together... That's how the trouble started... I was mad at you,
you see... Flaming... You know what I mean...

(TO SHIRLEY) Doesn't want a flaming wheelchair... Not
flaming good enough for her... Wants a flaming rotten
miracle!...

	(TO SHIRLEY) What she say? That was going to be her last letter?... *(SCREWING UP THE PAPER AND THROWING IT AWAY)*... Good!
SHIRLEY:	What you doing now... Took us an hour to get you to write that...
DEREK:	I mean... It's *stupid*, isn't it?... Don't know why I started writing to her in the first place... Why can't she flaming walk, like everybody else?... I have to flaming pick on somebody to write to who can't *walk*... I mean... practically everybody in the whole flaming world can *walk*...
SHIRLEY:	Told you not to say you could help her...
DEREK:	That's good, isn't it? Do you not feel great, now... Having to sit down and write letters to India every flaming week... It's a relief, isn't it?...
SHIRLEY:	Do you know what got on my nerves about her... Way she keeps going on about holy places... This being a holy place... Look at it... Petrol tanks all over the place... Dog dirt covering the pavement...
DEREK:	Telling you... Can do nowt about nowt, can you?... Can't even do anything about me *Mam* and *Dad*, can I?... What does she expect me to do about her flaming legs, millions of miles away...
	(TO KAMALA) I was... I was dead rotten about you... The two of us were...
	(TO SHIRLEY) I'm not Jesus, am I?... I can't make flaming cripples walk on water!...
SHIRLEY:	I mean... It's her fault... It's like blackmail that, isn't it?... If you don't help me to walk, I'll stop writing to you... Big deal... Her writing to us...
DEREK:	What she wants is to write to the Million Dollar Man... To send her a couple of bionic legs...
	That's how I felt that day... The next day, at dinnertime... I don't know what it was... I mean I was finished with you, anyway, now, wasn't I?... Maybe it was the nice sunny day... I don't know... In the middle of messing about the playground, I said to Shirley... *(TO SHIRLEY)* I'm going to St. Paul's... You coming? *(STEPS OFF RUG)*
SHIRLEY:	Yeah... If you want...
DEREK:	*(TO KAMALA)* We went into the church... That's how all the trouble started... Shirley liked the big wooden Jesus hanging from the ceiling...

SHIRLEY:	Looks a bit like you, doesn't he?... Maybe you *can* make cripples walk, Derek, eh?
DEREK:	*(TO KAMALA)* She went a bit funny on me, to tell the truth... She bought this card with Bede's prayer on it from the old woman... And had this idea of saying it under the statue of Jesus...
DEREK:	Looks *stupid*, man. Standing under a statue, saying *prayers*...
SHIRLEY:	That's what a church is for, isn't it? Praying... Come in...
DEREK:	Nuh...
SHIRLEY:	Come on... Try it... I want to try it...
DEREK:	Please yourself...
SHIRLEY:	It's your flaming friend that wants to walk...
DEREK:	*(TO KAMALA)* Just to shut her up, I knelt with her under the statue of Jesus... It didn't do anything for me, that statue... *Or* the prayer...
	(BOTH RECITE PRAYER) I pray thee merciful Jesus, that as thou hast graciously granted my sweet draughts the word o thy Goodness, grant that I may come at length to Thee, the fount of all wisdom and stand before thy face forever...
DEREK:	Didn't even know what it means...
SHIRLEY:	It's nice...
DEREK:	I don't believe in God and Jesus... It's against science...
SHIRLEY:	I do. I felt *something*... When we were saying that... I definitely *felt* something...
DEREK:	*(TO KAMALA)* It would've been alright, if we'd gone off then... But Shirley drags me over to the altar... And I see this old chair...
	(TO SHIRLEY) What's that?
SHIRLEY:	It's a chair...
DEREK:	*(TO KAMALA)* Like that statue of Jesus did something to Shirley... that chair was working things with me... It was dead old... It was a special chair... We went back to the place where they sold books and stuff about the church... Shirley found this book...
SHIRLEY:	It's Bede's chair... That's why it's old... It does miracles like...
DEREK:	It's just a lump of wood, Shirley... How can it do miracles?... *(TO KAMALA)* I mean... I don't understand this... You see... I didn't believe that chair could do miracles... Can *you* understand that?... *I* flaming can't...

SHIRLEY: They used to cut chips off it... You put the bits into water... And drink the water... and you're cured...

DEREK: The rubbish some people believe in, don't they?... Let's have a look at it again...

(TO KAMALA) We went back to the chair... You could get to it, dead easy... Just behind the altar rails... And I had me penknife on me... Only trouble was the people in the church... And the old wife looking after the bookshop... She'd been looking at us, minute we walked in... Like we were going to have a stick up in the place...

(TO SHIRLEY) Shirley... You go back and chat up that old woman... Take her mind off me... Right?

SHIRLEY: You're not going to take a chip off that chair, Derek, man?

DEREK: I don't know... Just go and chat the old wife up, will you?

SHIRLEY: You don't believe in it... You said so...

DEREK: I *know*... Talk to the old wife, man... She's watching us... Hurry up... Be time we were back in school...

SHIRLEY: What will I say to her?...

DEREK: Ask her about her knitting or her rheumatism... or Jesus...

(TO KAMALA) I mean... To be honest with you... I've ripped off stuff from all kinds of places... supermarkets... Woolworths in South Shields... Stalls... Ten times harder than slicing a bit of wood off an old chair... Should've been a walkover, shouldn't it? I mean... there were three other people in the church... But they were all on their knees, praying away like mad, with their eyes shut... So... I took out me knife... I didn't even need it... Because when you looked close, there was a splinter on the leg... I just needed to break it off... I broke it off... Put it in me pocket... Was just going to close the knife... when this hand grabbed me...

VICAR: Stop that! What do you think you're doing! Stop that...

DEREK: *(TO KAMALA)* What happened, you see... Was there was this door. I hadn't noticed it... And it was *my* rotten luck, this Vicar comes out, the minute I'm holding up the knife, to nick a bit out of the chair... He's coming at me, ranting away...

VICAR: I am *sick*. I am *sick to the heart* of this mindless, senseless, useless destruction. Dear God!... I am so sick of this violence!

DEREK: *(TO KAMALA)* It was like, I mean, my lucky day... Somebody had broken in and knocked off a silver candlestick or something couple days before... I tried to explain to him...

123

DEREK:	Sir... I wasn't doing any harm, sir... I was just closing my knife... I was just looking at...
VICAR:	You must *know* this is a Holy Place, boy. You are in God's house. Does that mean *nothing* to you? Do you feel *nothing*? Coming into God's church?
DEREK:	Yes, sir... It's holy, sir... I know... Sir, it was a saint who lived here, sir.
VICAR:	Give me that knife.
DEREK:	I wasn't going to do anything with it, sir...

(TO KAMALA) I could see Shirley watching us... Just standing... frightened... White and kind of paralysed... |
VICAR:	*(WITH KNIFE)* Dear God, look at it! Do your parents know you carry weapons like this about you, boy?
DEREK:	Sir, it's not a *weapon*, sir. Sir, my Dad bought me it for Christmas...
VICAR:	For *Christmas*. Dear God in Heaven! Your *father* bought you a *weapon like that*... For *Christmas*!
DEREK:	Sir, it's not a weapon, sir. It's a knife. It's got a tin opener and a corkscrew... and a bottle opener... It cost seven pounds, sir...
VICAR:	*Seven pounds* for a *knife*!
DEREK:	*(TO KAMALA)* Shirley was still watching us... Standing there... Like she was trying to make up her mind what to do... Come and help me or run off... Could see it in her face... Standing there...
VICAR:	Listen, boy... I am not angry with you. Do you understand?
DEREK:	Yes, sir. *(TO KAMALA)* Could've *fooled* me...
VICAR:	I want you to tell me... What is your name?...
DEREK:	Brian, sir... *(TO KAMALA)* Taking no chances with a character like that...
VICAR:	Brian, why did you take your knife to that holy relic?
DEREK:	Sir, I wasn't going to do anything with it, sir.
VICAR:	Brian. You are not *listening* to me. You don't need to lie to me. *Listen* to me... *Listen*... Are you *listening*, boy?
DEREK:	Yes, sir... I am listening, sir... Sir... I was saying a prayer, sir... To help my friend in India, sir... She can't walk, sir...

(TO KAMALA) Flaming wouldn't *listen* to me. |

VICAR:	*Listen* to me, boy. I am not going to *punish* you. I am not *angry* with you... I want you to tell me... Whatever terrible things were in your mind when you lifted your knife to mutilate that holy relic...
DEREK:	*(TO VICAR)* Flaming *telling* you! I'm *not* flaming lying! I was flaming praying for Kamala to get better and flaming *walk* again!
VICAR:	*(HOLDING UP KNIFE)* With *this*? *Praying?*
DEREK:	*(TO KAMALA)* Shirley was still standing there... Watching us. Frightened. I mean... What could she do? The Vicar was ranting away... She was in the clear, wasn't she? No point in her mixing in with vicars and St. Paul's church and Bede's chair...
	(TO KAMALA) And it was time to get back to school, anyway... She just turned away from us and walked out the church... Without looking back...
VICAR:	*(GRABBING DEREK'S JACKET IN HIS DESPERATION TO MAKE SOME KIND OF CONTACT WITH THE BOY)* I'm *speaking* to you, boy! *Answer* me!
DEREK:	*(TO KAMALA)* He'd grabbed my jacket. Shouting into my face...
VICAR:	In the name of God, will you open your eyes and *see*, boy. Look at me... I want to help you. Do you understand what I am *saying*? You are in trouble... and I want to help you...
DEREK:	*(TO KAMALA)* And I just kind of blew up. I went mad. I pulled myself clear of the flaming vicar... and I did a really weird thing... *(PUNCHING VICAR WITH ALL HIS STRENGTH)* Punched him with all my strength... I kept hitting him... He just stood there... Doing nothing... Couldn't believe it was happening to him...
	(TO VICAR, SHOUTING) Get rotten *stuffed*... The whole *flaming lot* of you. I don't *need* rotten help... *You* flaming need help... I can *flaming rotten help myself*... The whole *lot* of you... Get *rotten flaming rotten stuffed!*
DEREK:	*(TO KAMALA)* And I ran out of the church... The Vicar was shouting after me...
VICAR:	Brian... Come back, boy... Come back here... For God's sake!
DEREK:	*(TO KAMALA)* But I kept running... Right out of the church-yard... All the way back to my house...
KAMALA:	*(TO DEREK)* After Miss Graham left me, that day, with your little piece of wood from the holy man's chair... and your letter... I was full of so much happiness... The Jesus woman,

	of course, she was downcast and miserable as ever... You know how she gets troubled about people...
GRAHAM:	This man, Bede... in Jarrow... He wasn't a saint, Kamala... He wrote things,... Histories... and lived a life of a saint...
KAMALA:	Look at you, Miss Graham... Nothing pleases you... You are never contented, lady... You are saying to me, all the time, nothing will come to help me from England... Not to hope for any help from the boy... And now he sends me this, you are still full of miseries and worries...
GRAHAM:	I say not another word...
KAMALA:	Good!
GRAHAM:	I leave you with your relic and I go... I hope it does work some miracle... You know I hope that... You deserve a miracle... Everybody deserves an odd miracle now and then...
	(KAMALA WAITS FOR A MOMENT, TO MAKE SURE GRAHAM HAS GONE. SHE TAKES THE RELIC AND TOUCHES EVERY PART OF HER LEGS WITH IT, THEN HER HANDS, WRISTS, ARMS, FACE AND BROW. *SHE POURS WATER INTO A BOWL AND LETS THE RELIC STAND IN IT FOR A MOMENT, THEN DRINKS IT.)*
KAMALA:	*(TO DEREK)* Drinking the water, it seemed to me some strange thing was happening to my body. It was a very good, happy feeling. Listen, for this feeling alone, it was worth sending me it. Though I am sorry you were thrown into trouble and you lost the company of your friend. No. Listen. I will be honest with you. This is the truth. I know it is stupid and you are thousands of miles away from me and for me to go to you is like a journey to the stars. But I will be truthful to you. I was pleased you had only me for your dearest friend and the girl was no longer your friend. I know this is very selfish of me—but I am very selfish. I had more joy from your last letter than from all your others, because this was only thoughts between you and me... and your friend had no share of them. I thought I should tell you this.
	(SHE TAKES THE RELIC AND LIES DOWN)
	Lying down, that night, it seemed to me I felt pulsing of the blood in my legs... Though I was not sure. I lay down to sleep with great happiness... I slept so well, when I woke up, my mother and sister were gone to their work... *(SHE SLOWLY SITS UP. FRIGHTENED. SHE LOOKS AT HER LEGS... STRETCHES A HAND TO CHECK IF THE MIRACLE HAS HAPPENED...)* Good then! We will see if this miracle has happened! I do not

believe it has happened!
(SHE FORCES HERSELF TO MAKE THE TRAIL, PUSHING HERSELF WITH HER HANDS TO RAISE HERSELF ON HER LEGS... FIGHTING WITH ALL HER STRENGTH TO STAND... BUT THERE HAS BEEN NO MIRACLE. SHE IS AS BEFORE. THE STRENGTH HAS NOT COME BACK TO HER LEGS. SHE GIVES UP OVERWHELMED NOW WITH TOTAL DESPAIR. SHE TAKES THE RELIC SHE HAS BEEN GRIPPING IN HER HAND AND BREAKS IT INTO SMALL PIECES, THROWING THEM OUT OF THE HUT... SHE SMASHES THE DRINKING BOWL. SHE PULLS OUT DEREK'S LETTERS AND TEARS AT THEM AS IF SHE IS TEARING AT DEREK HIMSELF, BUT THERE IS NO RELIEF FROM THIS HOPELESS DESPAIR. SHE LIES FACE DOWN ON THE MUD FLOOR.)

Vishnu. Take my spirit out of this body. *Now.* Do this. Look at me. Look at the sickness in my heart, Vishnu, and free my spirit from this body. I wish myself death. Do this, Vishnu... Vishnu, do this... Please... Take my spirit...

(SHE LIES THERE, WILLING HERSELF TO DIE. SHE SLOWLY RISES.)

(TO DEREK) I am not sure how long I lay on the floor, willing myself dead. But in the end, a great thirst came to me... *(SHE GOES OVER TO THE WATER JAR AND POURS HERSELF A DRINK OF WATER)*

(TO DEREK) The joy that came into me, drinking the water... When I had relieved my great thirst, it came to me that I was hungry... I had had no food that morning... *(GOES TO THE RICE POT... TAKES A PORTION OF IT AND BEGINS TO EAT...* *(TO DEREK)* And joy came to me, in the eating of that rice... There was peppers and onions in it... and spices... and the hot chili...
Now... This is the thing that happened next... I was sitting in the doorway... Still enjoying the taste in my mouth of my mother's rice and vegetables... I heard the morning's Rubbish lorries come in from the city... I crawled out of the hut, and joined all the others rushing to the dump, to see what treasures the rich people of Madras had thrown from their houses that day...

(SHE IS CRAWLING)
I was very lucky... They were tipping the rubbish not too far from my hut... What came into my mind was wheels... Many times, the rich people threw out old pieces of bicycles or baby carriages... I wanted to find wheels... If I could find wheels... and some wood... and rope... *(SHE CONTINUES TO*

CRAWL... FIGHTING TO REACH THE NEWLY TIPPED RUBBISH... STRUGGLING... BUT MOVING FORWARD ALL THE TIME... NOTHING IS GOING TO STOP HER...)

DEREK: *(TO KAMALA)*
I saw Shirley, a few days ago... Just after your last letter turned up... I told you her Mam moved her to another school... I saw her in the shopping centre... I wasn't going to speak to her... But I wanted to tell her about you, you see...

(SHIRLEY IS WALKING... DEREK APPROACHING HER... THEY PASS EACH OTHER... PRETENDING NOT TO SEE ONE ANOTHER... THEN DEREK TURNS BACK AGAIN...)

DEREK: Shirley... Kamala's got to school... She worked it out herself... You know... Made something out of wheels...

SHIRLEY: That's great

DEREK: Thought you'd like to know...

SHIRLEY: Yeah... I did...

(SHIRLEY AND DEREK ARE STILL STANDING... UNSURE WHAT TO SAY TO ONE ANOTHER NOW... DEREK MAKES THE FIRST MOVE.)

DEREK: See... you *(MOVING OFF)*

SHIRLEY: Yeah... See you...

(KAMALA IS ON HER OWN WHEELED PLATFORM... ON HER WAY TO SCHOOL... HER BOOKS STRAPPED TO IT... ONE OF THESE DAYS, GRAHAM MIGHT ORGANISE A WHEELCHAIR FOR HER... BUT FOR THE TIME BEING SHE HAS TO RELY ON HER OWN WHEELS... IT'S SLOW, ENERGY TAXING, BUT SHE IS MOVING...

KAMALA: *(TO DEREK)* I think that is good now... I mean between us it is good... It seems now we can write to each other as real friends... I want to talk to you... I want to share the things that have happened to me and I share them... I do not write to you any longer to beg you for miracles... and you do not write to me to tell me you are looking for miracles for me... I think that is good... Do you not think that is good?...

(KAMALA MOVES OFF ON HER WHEELS...)

DEREK: Yeah... It's good... ... UP MUSIC

THE END